The Founding of the
RUSSIAN EMPIRE
in Asia and America

The Founding of the

RUSSIAN

EMPIRE

in Asia and America

by JOHN A. HARRISON

University of Miami Press

Coral Gables, Florida

Endsheets are reproductions of an original early nineteenth century
map from *Cary's Universal Atlas of the World*, London, 1808.

The maps throughout the text were prepared expressly for this book
by Carol Levy and Al Mitchell.

To
George Lantzeff
and
Robert Kerner

Contents

Maps

The Founding of the

RUSSIAN EMPIRE

in Asia and America

Preface

The genesis of this short history lies in pure chance. In September 1941, I entered graduate study at Columbia University with a view toward working in Chinese. In December 1941, I left school to join the Navy. Because I had some knowledge of Chinese, the Navy placed me in an intensive Japanese course. From 1942 to 1946 I had much occasion to use Japanese, both written and spoken, and in addition I took what can best be described as a highly informal crash course in Korean. In October 1945, I was stationed in Japan as a staff member of the United States Naval Technical Mission. My duties were light, being only such translating and interpreting as were required from time to time by my superiors, and during that cold gray winter in Tokyo and Fukuoka I began the study of written Russian.

At the same time I began to think seriously of the future, and it seemed the natural thing to continue my barely begun graduate education when I was discharged. I had Cambridge University in mind and upon the recommendation and advice of people at Columbia, notably L. C. Goodrich, I applied for and prepared to enter Cambridge. I was not at all clear as to what I intended to do there, but it seemed logical and best to put to use my imperfect but reasonably adequate knowledge of languages in the service of my original interest in the history of Northeast Asia, an interest that had been intensified by participation in the great Pacific war. Thus far my course had been set through the chance intervention of war.

My final selection of a university was also due to chance. I entered not Cambridge but Berkeley. Like all veterans dis-discharged from the service, I was given thirty days of terminal leave. My wife and I spent our leave skiing in the Laurentians, and on our return through New York we visited Professor Goodrich and discussed my plans with him. He told me that if I were intending to continue my work in the oriental field, I could hardly do better than study at a school that had Boodberg and Lessing on its faculty. Since my wife is that rarest of creatures, a native-born Californian and the descendent of several generations of native-born Californians, this coincidence of a first-class faculty in my field of interest and an ambience both familiar and friendly determined me. My luck still held, for Berkeley admitted me as a graduate student on my own recognizance, waiving all the usual transcripts and recommendations. Whether this was simply a courtesy to a returned veteran or an administrative slipup in a postwar period, I shall never know. At any rate, I was and remain grateful for what happened. During my time (1946–1949) Berkeley, at least the three departments in which I studied (History, Anthropology, Oriental Languages), was in a golden age with many wise, kind, and experienced scholars. I remember with much warmth McCune, Brown, Kerner, Lantzeff, and Harper of History; Lowie and Olson of Anthropology; Ashikaga, Lessing, and the superlative Peter Boodberg of Oriental Languages.

The final act of chance came with the selection of my program of studies the first day I was on the campus. I had not the faintest idea what constellation of courses and seminars I wanted to or had to take. I had been four years away from academic work and practice, courses and catalogs. The system then at Berkeley was to place a graduate student pretty much on his own. My adviser, understanding my need for retraining, decided on the rather draconian procedure of putting me in a spectrum of work across a number of disciplines. Then since there seemed to be time and energy left over and he felt that I ought to do more, he told me that Professor George Lantzeff was introducing a course in the history of Siberia that ought to be interesting and asked if I wanted to take it. This course was the last link in the chain of fortune that brought me to the study of that great human adventure—the pioneering of Siberia. Although George Lantzeff taught only the single two semester course (the only course, I believe, ever taught in any U.S. university on Siberian history), he permitted me, after the first year, to spend another year in tutorial study with him. During this time he led me through major sources of Siberian history.

Lantzeff's course was an offshoot of the vision and determination of Robert J. Kerner, who in the 1930s had founded the Northeastern Asia seminar at Berkeley. Kerner was a devoted follower of the historical theories of Soloviëv and Kliuchevski. His own work on the expansion of Russia led him to see that its Asiatic expansion could not be properly understood unless it was thought about in conjunction with the domestic and foreign policies and problems of the countries and peoples with whom the Russian expansion came into contact and contention. Kerner's belief that the expansion of Russia, of China, and of Japan were the determinants of a great struggle to control Northeastern continental Asia led him to establish this seminar, whose continuing topic was to be this matter of expansion. Kerner hoped, I think, that his colleagues and students would produce basic monographic studies, especially bibliographical, that would launch a new school of history. It never quite worked out the way he planned. Kerner was a kindly man and deeply loyal to and supportive of his students. He was, however, a demanding man in a quest for perfection from his students. He was often at odds with his colleagues concerning the importance of the field of history he was pioneering. His failure to achieve in his department what he thought was the just priority for the study of Russia did not improve his view of things. His long-range hopes for the seminar were mainly vitiated by the lack of interest among students, for they shied away from what seemed an extraordinarily difficult and esoteric field of study. This was their loss, for Kerner and Lantzeff were opening the gate to a marvelously rewarding area of research.

The only publications under the rubric of the Northeastern Asia seminar as such were: Y. S. Kuno's *Japanese Expansion on the Asiatic Continent,* of which only two of the three volumes projected appeared, volume I in 1937 and volume II in 1940; R. J. Kerner, et al., *Northeastern Asia: A Selected Bibliography,* two volumes, 1939; and R. J. Kerner, *The Urge to the Sea: The Course of Russian History*, 1946; R. H. Fisher's *The Russian Fur Trade 1550–1700*, 1943; George G. Lantzeff's *Siberia in the 17th Century: A Study of the Colonial Administration*, 1946; and A. Malozemov's *Russian Far Eastern Policy 1881–1904 with Special Emphasis on the Causes of the Russo-Japanese War*, 1958, all first-rate works, inspired and supported by Kerner.

While Kerner continued, as far as possible, to direct his seminar students into topics dear to his heart, the Northeastern Asia project was pretty much a shadow by 1946. Yet it had established—if not a school—then a Kerner way of thinking; it had inspired half a dozen fundamental works; it established intellectual and procedural parameters for the study of Russian expansion; and it had given George Lantzeff the opportunity to organize his course on the history of Siberia.

George Lantzeff was a gentle person and a remarkably good teacher. His knowledge of the sources was immense and easily given. His sense of organization of complex materials was elegant. I learned much from him, not only of the expansion of Russia but also of scholarship. In the over twenty years since I have left Berkeley, I have enjoyed as an avocation the reading of books and sources that Lantzeff suggested to me. This present history claims no merit as a learned thesis or an original work, for it is based on the teaching of Kerner and Lantzeff fortified by my own reading. It is an introduction to the history of an empire and, hopefully, an interesting and accurate, brief impression of the flow of men and events that moved Russia east during the millenium from the ninth to the nineteenth century.

I hope the book will be as enjoyable to read as it was to write and that it will not merely be useful but that the sheer magnificent adventure of the Russian-Siberian story will grip some others as it has gripped me. If this happens, then this book, which was written in homage to George Lantzeff and Robert Kerner, will have accomplished its purpose.

Because this is a small book on a large subject it is important to understand the principle of its organization. The text has three major divisions: The Land and the People, The Gathering of Russia, and The Moving Frontier. This seemed the most logical and the simplest way to tell the story. In the creation and expansion of the Russian Empire in Asia and in North America, Nature played perhaps the greatest role. The tribes, the pioneers, the settlements, and the fringes of the great empires are almost lost among the mountains, rivers, deserts, and steppes. This is a history that cannot be understood only in terms of men, ideas, and institutions; societies, economies, and polities. One has to keep in mind the land and the sea—thousands upon thousands of miles of it—from the Dnieper River to the Urals, the Altai, the Pacific Ocean, the Aleutians and Alaska; from Alaska to Hawaii, China, Turkestan, and the Caspian Sea. Then it is necessary to relate the creation of the Muscovite, later Russian, state. There are three parts to this: first, the growth of a powerful heterogeny of Slavic duchies, principalities, and free cities from the Gulf of Finland to the Black Sea; then their destruction by the westward-moving empire of the Mongols based on Karakorum; and finally the gathering of a Russia into a single state powerful enough to direct the flow of empire eastward. This latter is regarded by some Russian historians not only as the regathering of Russia but also as Russia's laying claim to the old Mongol empire. Finally, the Moving Frontier relates the story of the pushing forward and consolidation of the frontier, stage by stage, from the sixteenth to the nineteenth century. The history ends with the reign of Alexander I in the early nineteenth century because the premise of the story has been realized. The Russian empire in Asia and North America has been founded and indeed has reached its zenith as far as size goes. It will later withdraw from North America in order to consolidate within continental Asia; the expansion of its borders and the consolidation of its conquest within Central Asia and the Caucasuses will go on during the nineteenth century as will the Great Game with England for control of the northwestern approaches to India. The struggle with China for hegemony over Manchuria, Mongolia, and Turkestan is still very much alive. The Russian Revolution presented the new Soviet government with fresh problems not only of the reconquest of parts of the old Russian empire in Asia but with new sets of problems and principles in dealing with the non-Russian people within the borders of the Soviet empire. But these are all part of another history.

Because this is not an analysis but a history of how the Russian empire came to be, I have selected one major theme—the drive across Northern Asia and the Northern Pacific. It is not an ecclesiastical history or a political history or a social history or a history of foreign affairs, although the Orthodox Church, the policies of Muscovy, the social classes of Russia, the treasury in St. Petersburg, and the agents of Chinese Emperors, Japanese Shoguns, and Turkish emirs all play their roles. Where the roles are explanatory of the theme they have been interwoven into the story. Those who taught me can bear no responsibility for mistakes in fact or interpretation. One cannot be sure they would have approved the entire text. They were severe masters. But the telling of the story itself would have pleased them.

JOHN A. HARRISON

Coral Gables, Florida
April, 1971

Part 1

The Land and the People

THE LAND

Siberia proper is bounded on the west by the Ural Mountains, on the north by the Arctic Ocean, and on the east by the Bering Sea and the Sea of Okhotsk, each of which is an extension of the North Pacific Ocean. Siberia is bounded on the south by south Central Asia. This southern boundary line runs from the mouth of the Ural River across the Khazak steppes to the Altai and Sayan mountain ranges, across Baikalia to the Amur River and to the sea. Siberia proper, however, is only a part—although a major part—of the great Eurasian plain, plateau, and mountain area within which Russia built the largest continuous dominion in the world. Eurasia is enormous. From the Pripet Marshes in the west to Vladivostok in the east is a distance of more than six thousand miles. From the Arctic north to the southern deserts is more than four thousand miles. Within that part of the plain which lies between the Carpathian Mountains and the Altai Mountains, there is no really defensible frontier. This single fact of nature has done more to determine the history of the Russians than anything else. The natural frontiers of the Eurasian plain are along its southern rim. These are, running eastward, the Carpathian Mountains, the Black Sea, the Caucasus Mountains, the Caspian Sea, the Ust Urt Plateau, the Aral Sea, the Kizil Kum, the Tien Shan range, the Altai-Sayan ranges, the Yablonoi range, the Stanovoi range, and the Pacific Ocean.

Within this setting developed one of the great and unknown imperial dramas of history. Stage would perhaps be a more appropriate term, for these great natural barriers are on the edge of a series of unbroken plains over which one can travel for weeks from the Polish frontiers to the Altai. The homogeneity of the Eurasian stage becomes most evident at the height of the winter when this whole vast territory, one-sixth of the world, lies beneath a single blanket of snow.

Within this vast complex of regions, the soil, climate, terrain, and rivers follow regional patterns. The most important is the river pattern, for the Russian state and empire was built around the river basins and moved to the east on and across portages. Hardly less important is the pattern of the grasslands from China to the Black Sea, for this steppe road, skirting the fringes of Iranian-Mesopotamian civilization, was the funnel of invasion from the east to the west.

From north to south, Eurasia divides into four general zones of terrain. The northernmost, running along, roughly, the sixty-fifth parallel from Anadyr Bay to Archangel, is the tundra or cold desert. Here the winter lasts as long as ten months and for weeks on end, night is continuous. The ground is permanently frozen and since during the brief thaws the water cannot penetrate the frozen ground, the land turns to swamp. Here, where only lichens, mosses, and scrub bushes survive, life is inordinately hard. To the south of this zone where scrub birch passes into pine forest comes the great Siberian taiga, or zone of coniferous forest. This runs from the tundra boundary to a line that starts at the great bend of the Amur River, passes just south of Lake Baikal, continues westward across the headwaters of the Enisei, Ob, and Irtysh rivers, and continues into European Russia to the region of Kazan, where it swings north to the Gulf of Finland. The Siberian taiga, lying at high latitudes and isolated from the moderating effects of any ocean, has extreme temperatures. The winters are long and cold and the summers are brief and hot. South of this great forest area and running from the upper Amur to the Hungarian plain is the steppe. This is one vast grassland whose eastern extension is the Mongol plains. The grassland's westward extension is the Pontic steppe north of the Black Sea, one of the richest stretches of soil in the world, marked by the

Ukraine and the Volga valley. In the more central part of the
zone are the Alpine valleys of the Altai-Sayan Mountains and
the great Khazak steppe that runs from Lake Balkhash to the
Caspian Sea. In this zone the winters are long and cold and the
summers short and hot. In winter, however, the ground is kept
warm by snow, and the spring rains soon promote the growth of
the tough grass of the plains. In the spring and summer the
steppe is a carpet of grass. In the autumn and winter the land
is desolate and brown. So arid is it that in a single day what
was green as far as a man can see changes to hay. Yet the land is
so fertile that after rains what was barren one day becomes a
carpet of grass the next. In the west the steppe blends into the
hot salt deserts of the Aral-Caspian region, and in the east the
steppe merges into the sand desert of the Gobi.

Passing across Eurasia from west to east, the most significant
feature of the land is its flatness from the Carpathian Mountains
to the Enisei River. The Ural Mountains form no real barrier,
being always passable and at no point higher than three thousand feet.

Across the plain between the Carpathians and the Urals are
broad and slow rivers that flow south to landlocked seas. From
the Urals to the valley of the Enisei River stretches the largest
level area in the world—the West Siberian Lowland. Crossing
this lowland from south to north are the two great rivers, Ob and
Enisei, each of which has a great net of tributaries. The forest of
the Ob basin is swampy and the thick undergrowth is almost
impenetrable. The Enisei valley is drier, has little undergrowth,
and is thick with larches, firs, and spruces. Southeast of this lowland is the Turgan plateau, which drops down to the steppe and
desert of Turkestan in the midst of which lies the Aral Sea.
West of the Aral Sea and stretching to the Caspian is the Ust
Urt plateau; south and east of the Aral Sea are the great sand
deserts, Kara Kum and Kizil Kum. In these deserts wherever
water is available for irrigation the land has proven fertile and
great cities have arisen at those points, but where there is no
water life is impossible.

From the Enisei River to the Pacific Ocean the terrain changes
and is almost continuously mountainous in character. The rugged
nature of this Central Siberian Plateau is moderated, however,

since much of the area is connected by east-west valleys that permit easy portages and sledge routes. Lying across this plateau and to the east of the Enisei is the Lena River, remarkable for its size and navigable length and, like the Ob and Enisei, flowing north to the Arctic. While this region has extremely cold winters, the dry climate makes the temperature endurable.

West of the Kolyma River lies the Anadyr Range. North of this range is the end of Asia, the Chuckchee Peninsula, and directly southeast of it is the great block of the Koryak Mountains from the south of which stems the Kamchatka Peninsula. Kamchatka is two great parallel mountain ranges stretching over seven hundred miles in length and containing active volcanoes. Rich in timber, furs, and fish, the climate is severe and marked in the winter by almost continuous snow blizzards. Across the sea of Okhotsk from Kamchatka is the narrow continental Okhotsk coast, steep, straight, and rocky. The southern end of this coastal plain is marked by the mouth of the Amur River, Siberia's only exit to the open sea. The Amur originates at the junction of the Shilka and Argun rivers and along with its tributaries has a total of three thousand miles of navigable waterways. The Amur basin is fertile lowland with warm, wet summers and dry, cold winters. To the south the Amur valley blends into the Manchurian plain. To the north the Amur is separated by the Stanovoi Range from the headwaters of the Lena. From the lower Argun River to Lake Baikal lies a great chain of mountain basins and valleys occupied by meadowland, steppe, and forest and cut by strong, swift rivers. This Transbaikalia area has cold, clear, dry winters and warm, dry summers with sufficient rain to make for rich agriculture. The Yablonoi Mountains are a part of this region. To the west of Lake Baikal the Sayan range divides the Baikal watershed from the West Siberian Lowland. Southeast of Baikal rise the Altai Mountains, which are separated from the Tien Shan range by the Jungarian gate, which, leading from the Mongol steppe to the Khazak steppe, opens Europe to Asia.

The Steppe Road West

Along the southern rim of the forests and riverlands of Siberia lie steppes and meadows from Transbaikalia in the east to the Carpathian Mountains in the west. Starting at the highlands of the upper Amur, the road west runs through broad open valleys

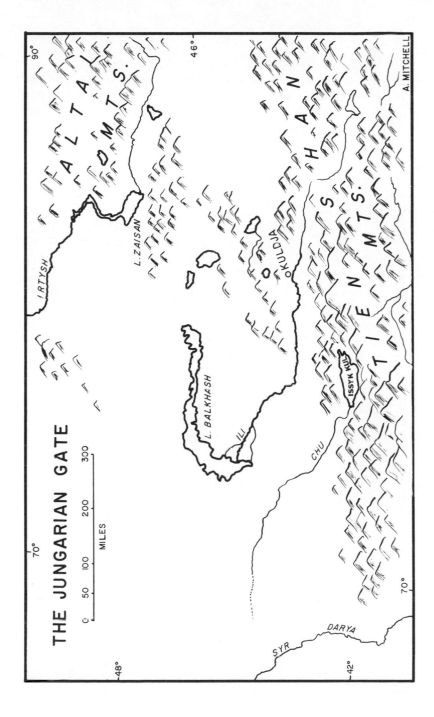

THE JUNGARIAN GATE

MILES
0   50   100   200   300

A. MITCHELL

and thickly forested hills and mountains to the plateaus and in-
termontane valleys of the Buriat-Mongol country south of Lake
Baikal. South of this lie the great outer Mongol plains that rise
to the granite slopes and snow peaks of the Altai-Sayan system.
Any nomadic movement starting in Outer Mongolia has a clear
run across the grasslands to the Altai-Sayan ranges.

Here the horseman may choose from several routes. He can
cross the foothills, which are highly suitable for horse and cattle,
and pass through the Alpine valleys to the west. He can turn
north into the lowlands between the upper Enisei and the Irtysh
rivers. He can take the more common path by turning south,
moving west between the Altai and the Tien Shan, and going
through the Ili passes (the Jungarian gate) to the Khazak
steppe, which runs uninterruptedly to the Caspian Sea and
then continues with no hindrance across the Pontic steppe to
the Carpathian Mountains.

This steppe land from Manchuria to Budapest has one thing
in common with the Arctic tundra. In both regions the earth and
nature impose an iron discipline that directs all life toward one
end. In the steppe the land and the weather made pastoral nomadism the only possible life. As the milleniae passed, the
herdsmen of the steppe, moving from water to water and grass
to grass, became a menace to the settled civilizations that arose
on the southern, eastern, and western peripheries of the steppe.
When the grass died and the oasis withered, the nomads raided
the agricultural surplus of their sedentary neighbors. The inexo-
rable demand for survival called for assaults against the settled.
What is not so clear is why for almost fifteen hundred years each
great assault was successful. The most probable explanation is
that the highly mobile, highly disciplined, self-sufficient, and
tough horse archer of the steppe was the most superior military
weapon created until the advent of the rifle and the cannon. The
cyclical attack through the steppe was the norm of the relation
between the nomad and the civilized. When the attack flowed
west to the great Russian plain north of the Black Sea, it set in
motion the history that this book relates.

The River Road East

A frontiersman moving eastward over the Eurasian river net

from Moscow or Vologda (the westernmost points of origin of the river road) would make his first stage that to the Ob River. From Moscow he went up the Moskva River to the Oka River and down that to the town of Nizhni Novgorod where he could make his way to the Kama River. He then went along the Kama to the town of Perm where the Kama joins the Chusovaia River and traveled up the Chusovaia to the Serebrianka River, where he made a portage to the Zherevalia River. He then entered a net of small rivers, the Barancha, the Tagil, and the Tura, which carried him into the Tobol River. He descended the Tobol into the Irtysh River and went down the Irtysh into the Ob River at Tobolsk. Starting from Vologda he had the choice of two river routes across the Urals, one north and the other south.

On the southern route he went along the Sukhona River to Totama and then traveled overland southeastward to Verkhoturie, the land gate to the Urals. At Verkhoturie he took the Tagil, Tura, Tobol, and Irtysh river route to the Ob. This trail contained the only long overland stretch on the eastward route. A frontiersman turning north instead of south from Vologda could go along the Sukhona River to Solvychegodsk at the juncture of the Vychegda and Northern Dvina rivers. He could then travel up the northern Dvina to the port of Archangel or travel along the Vychegda to Ust Nem where he would take the portage to the Pechora River. From the Pechora there were two possible routes. He could follow the Pechora to the Usa River and then, by way of the Usa, Elets, and Sobir rivers, turn the northern end of the Urals and come into Ob Bay. As an alternate route, he could leave the Pechora at the Schugar River and portage to either the Voliya River or the Iatrilia River, either of which would take him into the Sosva River, which flows into the Ob.

At Tobolsk, lying at the junction of the Tobol and Irtysh rivers, the pioneer heading for the Enisei valley stood at the end of the river route into the Ob basin. To the north the Irtysh joins the Ob, which then slowly flows north across a wilderness of forest and marsh, inundated in the spring and frozen in the winter, until it broadens into a great estuary and gulf that discharges into the Kara Sea. Eastward from Tobolsk there were

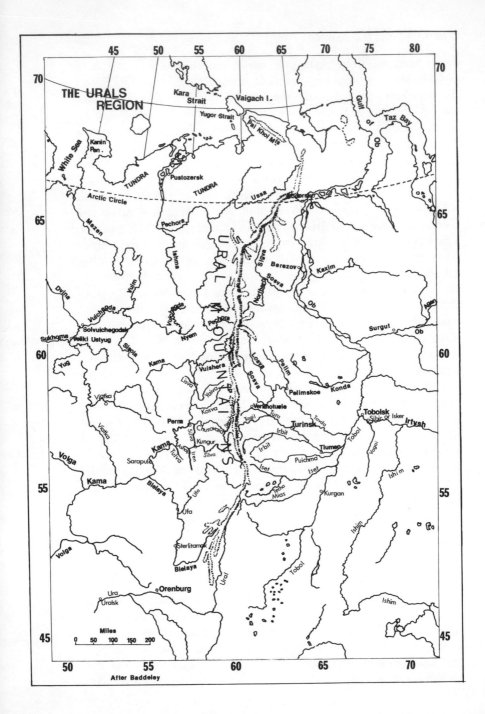

THE URALS REGION

two routes. He could either go north on the Ob into Ob Bay, passing the forts of Berezov and Obdorsk on the way, then down the Taz River to the great ivory and fur post of Tazovsk, later called Mangazeia. From Mangazeia on the Taz he would go up the Volochanka River to its source, make a short portage to the Turukhan River, and come into the Enisei River where the Turukhan flows into its lower course at Turukhansk. If he wanted to take the alternate southern route he had a number of choices. He went north on the Irtysh to its junction with the Ob at Surugut, then up the Ob to the Vakh River. From there he entered the Volochanka River and made a portage to the Chornaia River. From the Chornaia he reached the Elogui River, which flows into the Enisei. As an alternate route, he could follow the Ob to the Tym River, ascend that, portage across to the Sym River, and come into the Enisei. The most common route from the Ob to the Enisei, however, was to ascend the Ob to the Ket River, go up the Ket, and portage either to the Kas River or the Kem River, both of which flowed into the Enisei. The Ket River route was not only shorter but was guarded in its upper reaches by a fort at Makovsk.

The Enisei is a distinct boundary between the lowlands of West Siberia and the mountains of East Siberia. In the Enisei valley the pioneer was in much different country than that of the low-lying marshy Ob. The elevation is greater since there is a great escarpment along the eastern side of the valley that marks the beginning of a great and heavily forested plateau along whose southern rim great mountain chains lie. The climate is also different from the Ob, the differences in relief and precipitation resulting in exceptionally severe winters divided by brief, warm, dry summers. The upper and central Enisei, being largely mountain ridges and basins, have longer summers than the lower Enisei, and the tributary system connected this region with the rest of Siberia while the lower Enisei was a remote and forbidding region, particularly from Turukhansk to the Arctic Ocean. The Makovsk portage between the Ket and the Kem rivers led into the most important settlement in the Enisei valley, Eniseisk, built where the Upper Tunguska joins the Enisei.

From Eniseisk to the Lena, there were four routes that could be followed. The most common was the southern route along the

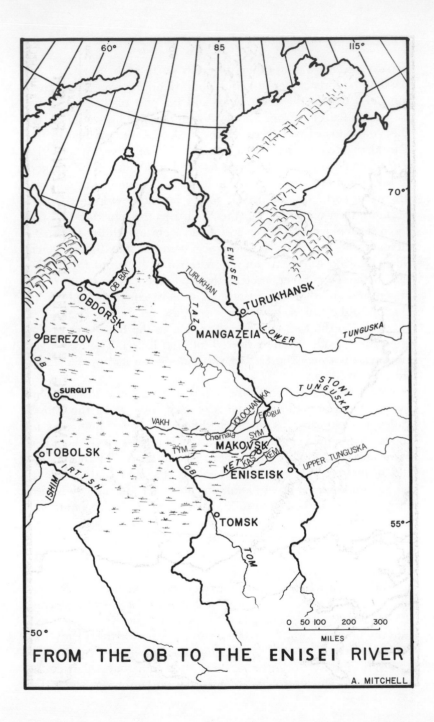

FROM THE OB TO THE ENISEI RIVER

A. MITCHELL

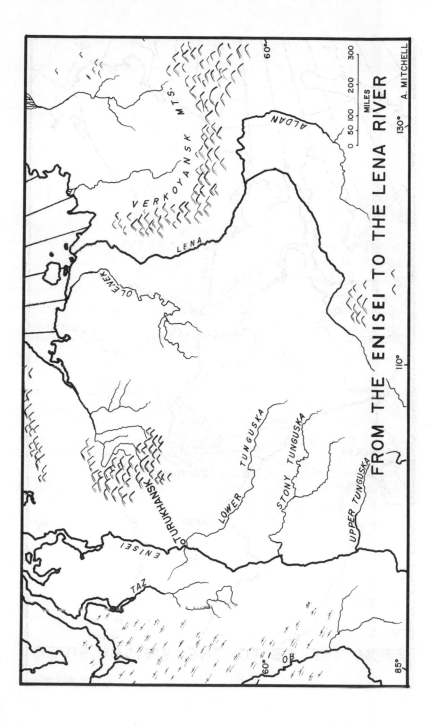

FROM THE ENISEI TO THE LENA RIVER

A. MITCHELL

Upper Tunguska to the Ilim River, then a portage to the Muka River, thence along the Muka, Kupa, and Kuta rivers to the Lena. This route was guarded at the portage by Ilimsk fort. The northern route started at Turukhansk and went along the Lower Tunguska to its source, then a portage to the Kulenga River and along the Kulenga into the Lena. If the goal was not the Lena system but Lake Baikal and the waterways leading from it, the frontiersman started from Ilimsk on the Upper Tunguska (here also called the Angara) and went along the Angara past the fort of Bratsk and into Baikal.

From the Baikal into the Amur valley was a relatively simple trip along the Selenga, Uda, Telemba, Chita, Ingoda, and Shilka rivers and into the upper Amur. For those far down the Lena River at Yakutsk, the trip to the Amur was better made by ascending the Lena to the Olekma River, then entering the Olekma's tributary, the Tugir River, crossing the Yablonoi mountains, going down either the Amazar or Urka rivers, and then entering directly into the Shilka River, which flows into the Amur. The route directly east from the Lena led from Yakutsk along the Aldan River to the mouth of the Maya River at Butalsk, thence along the Maya to the Ulya River or the Yudoma to the Arka River. Both the Arka and Ulya flow into the Sea of Okhotsk.

Northward to the mouth of the Lena lay the passage to the Arctic Ocean and along that coast one reached the mouth of the Yana River. From here the Indigirka, Kolyma, and Anadyr rivers can be reached by a series of very difficult portages through the Verkoyansk range or by coasting the sea rim from the mouth of the Yana to the east.

THE PEOPLE—THE SLAVS

That western portion of Northern Eurasia which lies between the Ural Mountains and the Danube River has known man and his works from paleolithic times, but our knowledge of those ethnic and linguistic groups in whom we are interested, the Slavs, is meager. We know that they were familiar with metal and metal fabrication. They were a patriarchal people whose groups of related families lived in communal villages (it was probably during their bronze age that they turned from nomadism to settlement) ruled by councils of elders. The land and its products were collective possessions of the village. They were good fighters with poor weapons. They kept bees, hunted, fished, farmed, and raised cattle. Since they were farmers and cattlemen they could not move as fast as the nomads who challenged and dominated them. In this disability and in the facts of the geography of Northern Eurasia lies the key to Russian history for a thousand years, and perhaps, for all of its span—the nomad penetration and conquest of the settled Russian civilization followed eventually by the Russian counterpush. From this action and reaction Russia perforce created an empire in Asia.

The origins of the Eastern Slavs (Russians) is as obscure as that of any peoples of Eurasia, but their European homeland probably lay between the Carpathian Mountains and the Dnieper River along the valleys of the Elbe, Bug, Oder, and Vistula rivers.

There is hardly any information on these peoples or their area from contiguous literate people. Their Roman neighbors had little contact with them, coming no closer to them than the frontier province of Dacia (Romania) established as a barrier against invasion of the Roman lines by Germans and Sarmatians. The Russians seem to have begun to drift slowly into the Dnieper and Dniester valleys of South and Central Russia between the third century B.C. and the third century A.D. They were pressured by the Asiatic Goths who, between the first and third centuries A.D., were organizing the Germanic tribes of South Russia and shouldering their way through the Slavs to the Roman frontiers. This slow Russian migration, which settled the Dnieper-Dniester valleys, was also due to the lure of the waterway system that linked the ancient trade between the Black and the Baltic and Mediterranean seas and the Black and the Caspian and Azov seas. The Black Sea trade terminals were dominated by the Greeks (at one time Athens got at least half of her corn and grain from the Black Sea region), who traded with whatever tribal empire dominated the steppes and the river mouths. From the eight to the second centuries B.C., the dominant tribesmen were the Scythians, a heterogeny of Central Asian peoples, whose founding of a conquest empire between the Don and the

Danube had wrecked the Lusatian culture of the Carpathian area and had contributed to the Slav migration eastward.

Since the Scythians had links with Western Asia, trading settlements arose on the Don, Dnieper, and Volga rivers connecting West Asia with the Baltic Sea. In the second century B.C. the Scythian steppes came under control of the Sarmatians, an Iranian group with some Mongol admixture, whose leading tribe, the Alans, gave their name to the entire tribal complex. The Alans had been pushed out of Asia by the powerful Hsiung-nu (Hun) federation that was to be pushed out of Asia by the Chinese Empire in alliance with Hsiung-nu enemies. Part of the Huns regrouped. They moved westward under the leadership of the house of Attila, broke into the Pontic steppe, defeated the South Russian tribal state of Ermaneric in 370–376 A.D., and pressed on into Europe.

During all these centuries of war and migration the ancient riverine trade passed through the Slav settlements of the mid-Dnieper region, but the mouths of the rivers were under the control of others. When the Hunnish state broke up and the Huns retreated eastward after the death of Attila and when the German tribes began to move from South Russia toward the Danube, the Slavs had an opportunity to migrate into the Black Sea rim and into the Balkans. This brought them into close contact with the Eastern Roman Empire in the fifth and sixth centuries A.D.

The possibility that the Russians might have been assimilated into the Byzantine Empire was ruined by the incursion into South Russia of the Avars who forced the Slavs back up the Dnieper River. The Avars, driven from their own homeland, passed across South Russia into Hungary and spread as far as France, where their spearheads were beaten back by the Franks in 565 A.D. They retired to Central Europe, centering their power on Dacia and making unwilling allies out of the Slavs. The subsequent destruction of Illyricus (the region from the Alps to the Peloponnesus) by the Avars with Slav help changed history. It destroyed the physical and cultural bridge between Rome and Constantinople and brought about great changes in the political life of the Slavs, for the Turkish Bulgars, infuriated by Avar raids, drove the Avars out of the lower Danube region and the Balkans (635–641), and the Turkish Khazars drove them out of South

Russia (686–720). (The last Avar remnant in Eastern Europe was defeated by Charles the Great in 796). This Bulgar-Khazar conquest of the Avars liberated the Slavs from the domination of steppe nomads for the first time in centuries, and they began to expand into their old lands. The Bulgars, who might well have replaced the Avars as rulers of Southern Russia, were pushed into the Balkans by the Khazars, who not only left the Slavs alone but brought them into the rich Volga-Dvina trade.

These Turkish-speaking Khazars had originally been part of a Tungus federation, which, like all nomad federations, had broken up and the Khazars had taken the well-worn path east to the Pontic steppes. The Khazars, however, had abandoned nomad ways in favor of trade and settlement after their conquests of Georgia and Armenia in the seventh century. By the early eighth century the Khazars controlled a state that ran from the Amu-Darya River to the middle Dnieper River and which had its capital at Itil on the Caspian Sea. The Khazars were friendly to the Slavs and were for them both a barrier behind which they were safe from nomad invasion and a link between the growing Slav trading towns and the wealthy, civilized, and productive khanates of Central Asia such as Merv and Bokhara. It was during the eighth and ninth centuries and under Khazar aegis that the Slavs migrated into areas as far apart as Brandenburg Prussia and the Balkans.

It was in the ninth century that separate Slav states, such as those of the Poles, Prussians, and Czechs, began to form. The main state was that of the Russians, a loose federation of the trading communities of Kiev, Novgorod, Pinsk, Chernigov, Polotsk, and Smolensk. These cities were the political centers from which grew the first Russian state under the leadership of Norse adventurers. The Khazars and the Bulgars were the only invaders who stopped on the fringes of the Slav steppes instead of passing across and therefore they had great influence on the development of Slav history. Both groups had close connections with Baghdad. Emergent Russia was therefore on the verge of a Moslem world that could easily penetrate Russia through the Caspian and the Volga. The Eastern Slavs were not incorporated into the Islamic world largely due to the fact that the Scandinavians had welded the Eastern Slavs into a bloc of their own.

Kiev

The first of the Norse military brotherhood or Varing (Slav *Variagi,* Greek *Varangoi*), commonly called the Rus, began to appear in Russia in the eighth century, groups of them taking the route of the Baltic, Dvina, and Volga rivers to the Caspian and later the route of the Neva, Volkhov, and Dnieper rivers to Constantinople. These men were freebooters who sold their armed services to the Slav merchants of the Dnieper towns and often became the rulers of the communities they served. According to tradition the first Norse ruler of a Russian town was Rurik, who established himself in Novgorod. Two of Rurik's retinue moved down to the Khazar outpost of Kiev, which they reduced to submission. It was one of them, Oleg, who formed the first Russian state. In 879 he brought both Kiev and Novgorod under his rule. Kiev began, under him, to play the leading part in this loose federation of towns and cities. By the end of the ninth century Kiev was the acknowledged leader of the other duchies, principalities, and free cities of the Eastern Slavs and a great commercial center linking Europe to Constantinople and the East on a route that was not subject to Moslem interference. It was Kiev under Oleg that mastered the north shore of the Black Sea and secured *de jure* recognition of the Slavic state from the Byzantine Empire.

In 913 a Varangian group from Kiev, desirous of securing wealth in Central Asia, passed through the Khazar state by permission. Instead of continuing to their announced destination, they plundered the area around modern Baku. On their return the Khazars met them at the Volga and defeated them. In 943 another Kievan band raided into the Caucasus and again the Khazars punished them. These Varangian aggressions against the Khazars demonstrate the growing weakness of the Khazar state. It was the fourth Kievan prince, a man of Varangian descent but with a Slav name, Sviatoslav, who extended Kievan power over the lower Don and to the Volga. He mounted the first Russian counterstroke against the nomad, an action as initially successful for Kiev as it was to be ultimately disastrous.

Sviatoslav of Kiev (regarded by Soviet historians as the founder of Russian foreign policy) nursed ambitions to create a military empire that would embrace the Eurasian waterways from the Danube to the Caspian. To this end he struck toward Asia and toward the straits, subjugated the upper Volga valley, and attacked the Khazar state. Following the destruction of the Khazars he conquered the northern Caucasus and then turned to the lower Volga where he seems to have wanted to establish his capital while he adopted the Khazar title *kagan* (chief of state) as did his successors. Meanwhile, a powerful Bulgar state under Simeon was expanding. As the Bulgar conquests neared Constantinople, the worried Greeks turned to Sviatoslav as an ally and offered him a subsidy and whatever he could seize in Bulgaria. Accepting this opportunity, Sviatoslav turned from his campaigns in the Lower Volga toward the Balkans. By a light-ning-like campaign he established himself on the Danube in 967.

The Greeks, now threatened with a powerful Kievan state on their borders instead of the Bulgar one they had schemed to destroy, entered into an alliance with the nomad Pechenegs of the trans-Volga, who attacked Kiev while Sviatoslav was in Bulgaria. Sviatoslav's diplomacy, however, was equal to his military ability. On his return home to relieve Kiev, he entered into an alliance of his own with the Pechenegs, turned back toward the Danube, picked up the Magyars as allies on the way, and swept the Balkans like a rake of fire. The Greeks, who by their own diplomacy had created this formidable power on their frontiers, now attempted to negotiate Sviatoslav out of the Balkans. Failing to do so, they abandoned talk for action. Under the brilliant gen-eral John Zimisces, they defeated Sviatoslav and concluded a treaty (971) that permitted Sviatoslav to return to Kiev. He was murdered on the trip back by his Pecheneg allies. The net results of the military campaigns of Sviatoslav were disastrous. The over-expanded Slavic states on the Dnieper had been exhausted by war. The defeat of the Khazars unblocked the way for a new invasion of Russia from the steppe, an advantage taken by the Polovtsoi (Cumans, Kipchaks), who invaded and dominated the Black Sea steppe for a century and a half. In 1054 occurred the first meeting between the Slavs and the Polovtsoi. In 1061 the first great raid came, and between 1061 and 1210 there were fifty large-scale invasions of Russia by Polovtsoi.

Vladimir and Yaroslav, the successors of Sviatoslav, gave the Kievan state relative security and a workable economy but per-

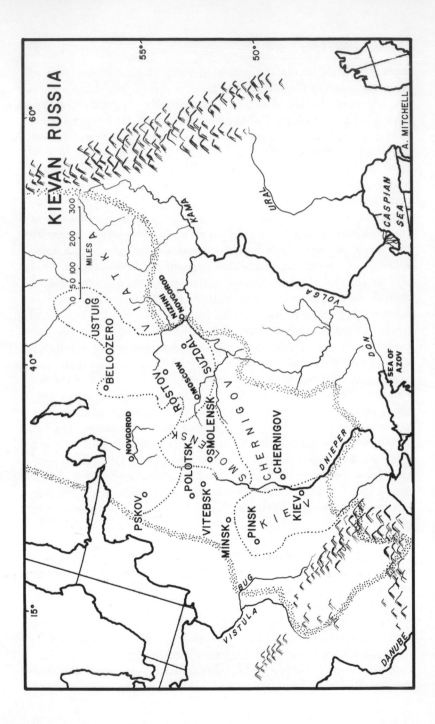

KIEVAN RUSSIA

haps even more important was the inauguration by Yaroslav of
the principle of inheritance in the succession to the throne of
Kiev. Yaroslav (1036–1054) gave a principality to each of his five
sons. The elder received the preeminent title of prince of Kiev,
thus beginning a long series of disastrous dynastic struggles, for
the Russian princes, regarding their domains as the common personal property of all descendents of Yaroslav, rejected the idea of
passing all of the domain to one member of the family. All heirs
got a share and the sons, in order of their age, received the cities
of the domain in order of their importance. The subsequent
death of an heir moved all the heirs upward in the same order
and the appanages shifted to the remainder in order of importance. This created an impermanence of rule that led to bad
government and exploitation. As the generations passed it led to
internecine warfare, the atomization of the Kievan state, and the
decay and eventual ruin of Russia.

This chaos in government reached its suicidal peak in time to
render a maximum advantage to incoming nomads, particularly
since the various Russian princes tended to form alliances with
groups such as the Polovtsoi against their nearest princely neighbor, thus opening South Russia to any and all who wished to
come in. Indeed, to any and all who wished to get out, for this
constant princely strife led to a peasant migration to the west of
Russia. The one great exception in that he sought union instead
of personal power was Vladimir II Monomach (1113–1125), who
successfully fought the Polovtsoi and convoked a congress of the
princes of Russia to discuss the Polovtsoi question. Vladimir
persuaded the princes to unite, and one of the great (but soon
forgotten) lessons of early Russian history was learned when the
united princes beat the Polovtsoi, proving that without the disruption of political dissension Russia could beat the nomads.
With the death of the Monomach there was no one left to enforce the lesson. A period of instability began, marked by a great
migration from Kiev to Southwest Russia (Galcia-Volhynia) and
to Northwest Russia (Novgorod), for the Polovtsoi were again
raiding the Kievan area. The effect of these attacks was to crum-
ble the Kievan state into separate independent principalities.
Some new cities arose as Kiev itself declined (it was sacked in
1169 by Andrew of Suzdal and in 1203 by the Polovtsoi led by

Russians). There was a brief resurgence under Rostov-Suzdal and Novgorod, but it was too late. Kievan Russia was now almost through. Exhausted by wars and dissension, with the great commercial base of Constantinople cut off by the Crusades, and with a harassed population fleeing to the north and the northwest, it was a mark for invasion at a time when one of the greatest of nomad movements was getting underway.

The Mongol Invasions

This nomadic movement was a fruit of the great federation of Turkic people led by the Baikal Mongols under the leadership of the house of Genghis Khan. It was formed from the shreds of three nomad political states: the Uighurs of Jungaria, the Khalkas of South Siberia, and the Khitans of Manchuria. At its height, it was composed of six major groups of whom only one, the Mongols of the Onon, Selenga, Orkon, and Kerulen rivers (systems which drain into Lake Baikal or the Amur River), was truly Mongol.

In the middle of the twelfth century there existed no strong state between the Urals and the Chinese Empire, and the area from the Great Wall of China to the Urals was at the mercy of anyone strong enough to command it. Since there was no national consciousness among the tribes and the pastoral nomads had a common internal organization and culture as well as a common interest in pasture and spoils, an extraordinarily able man could unite these disparate groups into a conquest empire. This was done by Temuchin (Genghis Khan, 1155–1227), who first turned his tribal league against North China. Once assured of the conquest of this vast (but at that time decentralized and weak) state, the Mongols, with invaluable military experience and Chinese aides and techniques, turned south and west. With a tough and self-sufficient cavalry army bound together by an iron discipline, practicing group responsibility, and demonstrating a deliberate policy of terror to reinforce their aspects of invincibility, the Mongol cavalry divisions moved from China into Central Asia.

The civilized states of central Asia with their great cities were utterly destroyed, their irrigation systems were smashed, and the land became desert. The rise of the Mongol empire brought about a great shifting of populations in Asia. It is worth noting that Siberia became a land of escape for those tribes who wished to flee the whirlwind. This altered the primitive cultures of Siberia, i.e., the Turkish Yakuts moved north to the Lena River area.

In 1223 an advanced patrol of Mongol horsemen appeared in the southern steppes. At the point where the Kalka River empties into the Sea of Azov, the Russian princes, disunited as usual, met the Tatars and were utterly defeated. The victorious Tatars withdrew behind the Urals, however, and this one catastrophic appearance seemed for a while to be merely an episode, although a terrible one, in the ancient struggle with the steppe. The reprieve was short. In the last autumn of their existence the princes of the degenerating Russian states did not bother to effect any plan of concerted action against any disaster that the Tatars' ominous silence might portend.

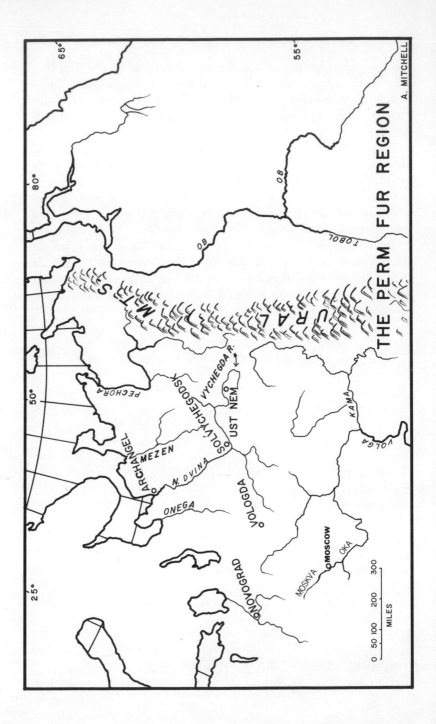

THE PERM FUR REGION

A. MITCHELL

65°
55°
80°
50°
25°

OB
OB
TOBOL
URAL MTS
PECHORA
VYCHEGDA R.
SOLVYCHEGODSK
UST NEM
ARCHANGEL
MEZEN
N. DVINA
ONEGA
VOLOGDA
KAMA
VOLGA
NOVOGRAD
MOSCOW
MOSKVA
OKA

MILES
0 50 100   200   300

Part 2

The Gathering of Russia

By the time of the death of Genghis Khan in 1227, the Mongol Empire stretched along the fifty-fifth parallel from the Urals to the Pacific Ocean and included North China and Central Asia. When the great Council met after the death of Genghis, the empire was broken into a number of component parts called *ulus* and portioned among each of Genghis' sons by his first wife according to Genghis' wish. The area from the Urals to the Dnieper was given to the eldest son, Juchi, but Juchi died and his inheritance passed to his son, Batu. In 1236 Batu crossed the Urals to conquer his new domain, bringing twelve divisions of cavalry under the great general Sabutai. Between 1236 and 1240 Sabutai defeated North Russia and literally crushed South Russia. By December 1240, when Kiev was taken, the conquest was complete. After an extended raid into the vicinity of Vienna (in the course of which the Polish and German forces of Central Europe were heavily defeated) Batu retired on receiving news of the death in 1241 of the great Khan Ogotai (son of Genghis and his successor as khan) and settled his capital at Sarai on the lower Volga. This new state of Batu, which encompassed the steppes of Southern Russia and the forests of Central Russia, was known by the Mongols after the name of Batu's army as the Khanate of the Golden Horde. Since Batu's domain was in theory at least a part of the Eurasian Empire ruled from the Mongol capital of Karakorum, Russia became, in a sense, connected with all Eurasia. The ancient Slavs' struggle to preserve themselves from the ceaseless erosion of the steppe nomads ended in the terrible defeats of 1236 to 1240. Russia was scattered, her various rulers had to be confirmed in their status by the edict of a Mongol khan at Sarai, and that khan was to play a significant part in the destinies of Russia.

Moscow

It is not the purpose of this book to enter into any extended description of the Mongol occupation of Russia or of the enormous political, cultural, social, and economic consequences of that occupation. The effects of this domination in Russia were to be felt for centuries after that yoke had been broken. For our purposes it is sufficient to note the deep scar left on the Russian mind by the failure to have defensible borders against the nomads and the unconscious national desire to end this situation by pressing back the nomad permanently.

The nature of Tatar authority varied from region to region in Russia, but the universal interest of the Mongols was in the collection of taxes laid on the various states. Originally the collection of these taxes was in the hands of Tatar officials, but by the fourteenth century the various Russian princes were delegated this responsibility. The diligent pursuit of this obnoxious duty by one clever grand duke, so indefatigable in his financial responsibilities that he informed the khan of the delinquencies of his fellow rulers, was to be the initial lever in releasing Russia from the Mongol trap.

Ivan Kalita, who became grand prince of Moscow, a rather inconsequential town in 1328, ingratiated himself with the Mongols. Attracted by the ensuing peace of the city, many colonists came into the Muscovite principality. This is the beginning of the growth of Moscow. Kalita was judged by the khans as being the Russian ruler most amenable to the overlordship of the Horde, and he was made grand prince of all the Russians. Kalita's descendants continued his policy of cooperation with the khans. The territory of Vladimir was awarded to Kalita's son by Uzbeg Khan (1314–1341) and the Russian capital was moved from Kiev to Vladimir.

The rule of Uzbeg marks the zenith of the Golden Horde. It was now a power as respected as it had been feared. It had established diplomatic relations with the Papacy and with the western states. It had a trade so considerable that Italian merchant colonies were established in South Russia. Islam became the state religion of the Tatars under Uzbeg. The Horde maintained, however, the usual religious tolerance of the nomads. The peace attained by Uzbeg was continued by his son Janibeg, who confirmed the privileges granted by his father to the Russians and granted great privileges to the clergy. Ironically the entire Russian policy of the Horde supported the two forces that were eventually to emancipate Russia from its overlordship. The one was the city and state of Moscow, which was to lead the struggle against the Tatars, and the other was the Orthodox clergy who were preventing any assimilation with the invader. The two united when the metropolitan of Russia moved from Vladimir to Moscow and lent his enormous prestige to that city. Moscow was already fortunate among Russian cities in that it was not fragmented and was usually ruled by one man who was capable.

The first great challenge to the Tatars came from Dmitri Donskoi, grandson of Ivan Kalita and grand duke of Moscow (1359–1389). In Dmitri's day the political power of the Horde was being weakened by numerous internal conspiracies for power and leadership as well as by unruly Tatar nobles who raided and terrorized the tax lands of the khan. When Dmitri of Moscow stopped a punitive raid into his territory, it was decided, albeit somewhat reluctantly, to punish him. Mamai, khan of the Golden Horde, formed his armies and invaded Russia in 1380. Dmitri called on the Russian princes to make a stand, but hardly any of them answered the call. At Kulikovo Meadow on the upper Don, on September 8, 1380, Moscow fought, almost alone, a successful battle which was a decisive defeat for the Horde. The psychological effect of this victory on Russia was enormous. The Tatars no longer seemed invincible. The people began to look on Moscow as the deliverer and the liberator of Russia. But the victory was short-lived. Timur Leng (Tamerlane), Emir of Transoxiana, who was a Turk and not a Mongol, had decided to assert his authority over the Horde. He dispatched his vassal Toktamysh to invade Mamai's lands. Toktamysh took over the Horde. To reestablish its authority, he decided to break Dmitri's *later* power. The unprepared Dmitri fled, and Toktamysh devastated Eastern Russia and seized Moscow in 1382. This restoration of absolute Mongol power lasted only until Tamerlane turned against his too powerful vassal and destroyed him in 1391–1395. After this the Horde broke up into dissenting groups, but its strength was still sufficient to prolong the nominal Mongol yoke in Russia.

Novgorod and Perm

To the north of Moscow lay an area untouched by the Mongol invasions. The center of this area was the city of Novgorod whose fur hunters with their exploitation of the Lake Ladoga, Valdai, and Kama river area were to carry Russians into the Urals by way of the Dvina and Pechora rivers and the Arctic Ocean. This rich fur territory, which lay between the Dvina and Pechora rivers and which was known as Perm, was crisscrossed by a net of portages. Novgorod itself was a considerable trading city by the time of its first mention in the Chronicles during the ninth century. The extent of its incursion into Finnish territory can be seen by the mention in the Chronicles of fur outposts at Rostov and Belo Ozero. The Chronicles mention a victory of the Yugrians over the Novgorodians at the Iron Gate in 1032. This indicates that Novgorod's people were already on the northwest slopes of the Urals in that early century, for the Iron Gate was probably at the headwaters of the Pechora River where the Urals can be crossed to reach the mouth of the Ob.

When Scandinavians established themselves in Novgorod in the ninth century, it was just one of the trade centers of the new Kievan state. By the end of the eleventh century Kiev granted Novgorod a charter, making it a free city. This relative autonomy was granted for military help received by Kiev, and it gave Novgorod the right to accept or reject the deputy of Kiev. With the periods of civil war in Russia after the death of Yaroslav, Novgorod had by the twelfth century become an independent republic headed by a nominal prince. The base of all power in the city was the Veche, a general male assembly of the heads of families. The Veche deliberated on proposals submitted to it by the city council, which consisted of the most prominent men of the city. All grave decisions, including the making of war, were decided by male plebiscite. The city was administered by two elected officials; one was the civilian mayor and the other was in charge of the troops of the city. Over all of these men and groups was the figurehead prince. In actuality, the government of the city was in the hands of the wealthy merchants.

In 1096 Novgorod's merchants sent an expedition to the Pechora River. This group went into the Yugra country (that land immediately west of the northernmost spur of the Urals). They heard from the Yugrians that farther to the east and to the north were impassable mountains, a strange people, and a wealth of furs. This expedition marked the beginning of an increased activity in the fur region by Novgorod. As increasing civil war in the Kievan state blocked the southern trade routes, Novgorod turned more and more to the Baltic trade. She joined the Hanseatic League in the thirteenth century and became the chief supplier of furs to Europe. As her fur trade grew, so did her settlements along the Sukhona and Dvina rivers. The suppliers of the trade were Novgorodian freebooters who operated in the forests and streams of the Dvina country and among the Finnish tribes of Yugra (the Ostiaks, Voguls, and Samoyeds). In the twelfth century a large party of Novgorodians descended the Kama River to the Volga. Some stayed at the Kama mouth to found a settlement. Others ascended the Vyatka River to a large Finnish settlement that they captured. Later both groups joined forces at what was to become the city of Vyatka, which became the center for the Novgorodian colonies of this area. These colonies were self-governing and generally defiant of the authority of the mother city. The entire net of fur posts in the Perm region became a sort of petty state, unique in Russian history because it had no prince.

The prosperity of Novgorod, based on her trading empire, excited the attention of other Russian states, in particular the ancient cities of Rostov and Suzdal. These cities, headed by able princes and increasing in size through the emigration of persons unhappy with the internal wars of Kiev, became increasingly envious of Novgorod. In the twelfth century, a Suzdal colony was established at Ustiug on the Sukhona River along the main road to Yugra, and Vyatka and Belo Ozero came under the domination of the Volga states. In 1169 the prince of Kiev and

Suzdal, Andrei, sent agents to stir up a rising among the Permian colonies and then launched an attack. The attack was a failure. The colonial unrest subsided and Novgorod seized Suzdal's fur colonies as reparation.

The rulers of Moscow then began to wage war with the city of Novgorod in order to gain control of the fur trade and the routes to the fur country. One result was that the princes of Moscow began to create a little colonial empire of their own between the Kama and the Urals and at the same time to seize land in the Oka River. This Volga colonial attempt was interrupted by the Mongol invasion, but the Novgorodian fur empire remained untouched, and it was during the Mongol period that Novgorod expanded its colonies and joined the Hanse. In the thirteenth and fourteenth centuries Novgorod held the balance of power in the struggle among the various Russian princes for the title of grand prince of the Russians. This balance was only ended when Yuri of Moscow became the grand prince and founder of the Muscovite line in 1320. With the accession of Yuri, the throne of Moscow became a grand principality. Also with his accession a peace descended between Novgorod and Moscow. Yuri even aided the Novgorodians against the Swedes and personally led an expedition against the pirates of Ustiug. Yuri was assassinated in 1325.

His successor was Ivan Kalita who not only maintained the peace but, in character with his pacific position, even purchased the post of Belo Ozero from the city. Kalita's interest in Permia, however, was not so much due to furs as it was to the fact that the only sources of metals in Russia were the Novgorod mines in Perm. He claimed the mining colonies on the basis of some dubious charters. This chicanery failed but the cautious Kalita abstained from war. Instead, he attempted to create a sort of fifth column within the Novgorod colonies since the strife in the city of Novgorod between the people and the boyars had created a class of wandering exiles in the Dvina region that Moscow attempted to use for its own purposes. So a species of guerilla warfare succeeded the peace between Moscow and Novgorod. In 1363 Novgorod made its most ambitious attempt into the trans-Ural region. A group crossed the Urals, one part going down the Ob River to the sea and the other up the Ob to its headwaters.

They returned with enormous spoils and were attacked by the Muscovite colonists in the Dvina region. Novgorod retaliated by raids on the Volga region. At this time Dmitri Donskoi was ruler in Moscow, and he had to hold these raids off with one hand while facing the Horde with his main strength. In 1371 another city-state, Yaroslav, plundered Novgorod. The city had scarcely recovered when in 1386 Dmitri launched a successful attack against its colonies on the Dvina River. By the end of the fourteenth century a full-scale war was raging between Novgorod and Moscow for control of the Perm colonies. In 1393 Vasili I of Moscow seized Vologda and gained control of the portages between Novgorod and the upper Volga, enabling him to cut off the grain transport from the south. In retaliation Novgorod seized Ustiug. In 1397 Vasili led an expedition into the Dvina region in an attempt to gain the allegiance of the settlements there, a number of which went over to Moscow. Vasili's main appeal was to the merchants. They were promised their dignity, rank, and profits, a change from Moscow's usual policy of squeezing this class. Vasili even offered to free the Dvina merchants of taxes.

Novgorod's answer was a counter expedition to the Dvina lands, and all through the end of the fourteenth and into the early fifteenth century, the raids and counter raids continued. Then in the middle of the fifteenth century the balance of all power in Russia began to swing toward Moscow for the Horde broke into a number of smaller khanates, such as those of Kazan, Crimea, and Astrakhan. Some Tatar leaders entered the service of Moscow. With Mongol domination practically at an end, Moscow now began to put greater pressure on Novgorod. The final conquest of Perm came during the reign of Vasili II (1425–1462).

The early reign of Vasili II was a period of insecurity for Moscow. His uncle Yuri claimed the throne, and for a number of years the position of Vasili II was insecure. This gave Novgorod a breathing space. It stayed neutral over the struggle in Moscow and this paid off as Vasili, out of desperate gratitude, once promised to return all lands seized and actually did return Vologda.

At the same period of time, Moscow was being roughly handled in the Perm region by a part of the Golden Horde that had settled at the confluence of the Volga and Kama in an area called Kazan. This Khanate of Kazan now blocked Moscow's access to Perm. Vasili II tried to drive them out in 1445. He was defeated, captured, and only released on the payment of a large ransom. The ransom was raised by extorting tribute payments from the Muscovite people. Since it was generally held in Moscow that Vasili favored Tatars over Russians and that his campaigns were folly, he became enormously unpopular and was forced to flee his own city. He was recaptured, blinded, and sent to rusticate in the settlement of Vologda. In Vologda the blind man raised an army and, joined by his loyal Tatar allies, marched on Moscow and regained his throne. In recognition of Tatar services he granted land on the Oka River to his Tatar ally Kasim. In 1446 he formally recognized this gift as the Tatar Khanate of Kasimov, a bold and wise move that placed a loyal Tatar vassal force on the Moscow frontiers.

Vasili II now turned his attention to Novgorod. Forgetting his former gratitude and spurred by the desire to seize the wealth of that city and unite the Russian lands under one rule, he launched an expedition in 1456. Novgorod, being at this time internally beset by a class struggle, was soundly defeated in the field. It surrendered on terms that (by the treaty of 1456) ended its existence as an independent city-state, placed its foreign policy and its domestic ordinances under the grand prince of Moscow, and laid a poll tax upon its inhabitants. The next step for Moscow was to seize the semiautonomous fur colonies of Novgorod. In 1459 Vyatka surrendered to a Muscovite force. With this action Moscow gained a strong hold on the old Novgorodian colonial empire. In 1470, under Tsar Ivan III (1462–1505), Moscow began the final subjugation of Novgorodian territory. The boyars of Novgorod had tried to recoup their waning power by offering allegiance to their powerful neighbor of Lithuania. Since this amounted to heresy as well as treason in the eyes of Moscow—Lithuania being Catholic (where it was not pagan)—Ivan launched a crusade against the city. Between 1470 and 1478, he made it completely subject to Moscow, diverted its wealth to his treasury, seized the Dvina colonies, and began Moscow's final absorption of Perm, that is, the region from the headwaters of the Vyatka, Volga, Pechora, and Kama rivers to the Urals—the heartland of the fur trade. In this area, it should now be noted, the Russian Church was playing an important role in Perm as was to be true with the entire colonization of Siberia.

Stephen, bishop of Perm, had learned the language of the Finns of Zyria and had gone to Rostov to prepare himself for missionary work in Zyria. He translated the Scriptures into Zyrian and then going into the field, founded a church at Yust Vym on the confluences of the Vym River. Though he was a Muscovite, Novgorod did not object to his work, and he made a number of converts and became established as bishop of Perm by orders of Moscow. He was popular with the natives because he protected them from Russian freebooters, and although his activities were entirely of a religious nature, they acquired a political meaning. By erasing religious differences, he brought the natives into near assimilation with Russians. His see of Yust Vym controlled a considerable territory and became a semisecular frontier mark of the Russian state. The bishops of Yust Vym thus became political rulers and levers of Moscow on the frontier. Yust Vym missions spread into trans-Uralia and the trans-Uralian Voguls raided in retaliation. In 1465 Moscow sent a retaliatory raiding force along the Pechora and across the Urals. In 1483 another Muscovite force got as far as the Irtysh River, returning with great spoils. These raids aroused the Perm natives and with their bishop as intermediary, they sent a delegation to Moscow to argue for peace in the region. The delegation was graciously received and their goodwill secured. The bishop of Perm was established as mediator for the tribal peoples, even outside the Perm area. The church thus paved the way for the extension of Russian authority in the region. Perm is an excellent example of religious activity transforming an area into a political base, a characteristic of Russian colonial policy as opposed to the colonial policy of other nations. Equally noteworthy is that Bishop Stephen's conversions were through the word and not the sword.

The Foreign Policy of Moscow in the Century Preceding the Conquest of Siberia

The great organized Tatar nomad encampments of Kazan and the Crimea not only constituted a menace to the orderly development of the Russian state, but they blocked vital river systems. Yet the very division of the old Golden Horde played into the hands of Moscow. Although Ivan III was still—as grand prince—nominally subject to the Horde, he did not, on his accession, request the khan for a charter confirming his investiture nor was he anything but negligent in paying tribute. As a punitive measure, the Horde launched an expedition toward Moscow (1465) but found its way there blocked by the Crimean Tatars on the lower Don River—a sign that the internal enmities of the Tatars would play into the hands of the rising Muscovite state.

About the year 1455 the khan of Kasimov entered into negotiations with the internal enemies of the khan of Kazan with a view toward making himself ruler of Kazan. He informed Ivan III of this, and the latter was overjoyed at the prospect of ridding himself of the Kazan menace and the roadblock on the way to Perm. In 1467 a joint expedition defeated Kazan and forced the city to accept peace on Russian terms. Meanwhile some Tatar nobles, disgusted with the endless internal strife of the various khanates and desiring to adhere to the better organized state of Moscow, began offering their allegiance to Ivan III. Naturally this attracted the attention of Akhmet Khan of the remaining Golden Horde, who resolved to punish his Moscow "vassal." Being able to campaign because he was at temporary peace with the Crimean Khanate, he moved in 1480 against Ivan III. The Russian and Golden Horde forces faced each other at the little settlement of Aleksin on the Ugra River for an entire summer. What followed was a Russian victory without a battle, for the Tatars, evidently not wishing to engage without promised Lithuanian aid which never came, withdrew. The Russians, no less loath to avoid battle immediately, followed suit. For the first time since the conquest of Batu, a Tatar force yielded the field without a struggle. With Kazan at peace under treaty and the Golden Horde obviously anxious to avoid a struggle, Ivan had a still greater piece of luck with the third great khanate, that of Crimea. Azi-Girei, khan of Crimea, had died in 1475, and at his death his khanate was shaken by the struggles between his six sons to succeed him. The eldest son fled to Polish protection and one of the younger sons, Mengli-Girei, took the throne and turned to Ivan as an ally. Ivan III and the Khanate of Crimea (which dominated the steppes from the lower Dnieper to the lower Don) thus became allies at a crucial moment in the history of the expansion of Moscow.

On the west Ivan faced the powerful Polish-Lithuanian state. Three-quarters of this state was composed of former Russian lands, as many Russian princes had become Lithuanian vassals rather than remain vassal to the Tatars. Lithuania therefore was fundamentally composed of a number of principalities who reserved the privilege of changing their allegiance. This was a fatal weakness. Although the real plans of Ivan have never been known, it can be assumed that he wanted to consolidate all the former Russian lands under one strong rule. His advantage in the west was in this peripheral weakness of the Polish-Lithuanian state. This advantage was reinforced by the preservation within the Lithuanian state of a spirit of Russian nationality by the Orthodox clergy. The Catholic-Orthodox struggles in Poland were reflected among the border principalities in a series of secession movements aided by Ivan. Meanwhile, Ivan's policy toward Kazan was aggressive. It utilized the Tatar enemies of Kazan and was aimed at unblocking the road to Perm. Ivan III was essentially a diplomat and not a warrior. His policy toward the Golden Horde was one of conciliation, yet he constantly probed to see how far he could go with neglecting his nominal duties as a vassal and his border governors had orders to strongly resist Tatar raids. The Horde was dissatisfied with Ivan, yet even while allied with Poland-Lithuania (which remained friendly with the Horde in order to keep an enemy at Russia's back), the Horde failed to act. This failure was not only due to dissension but to the greater danger the Horde faced in the enmity of the Crimean Khanate. Ivan pursued a policy of friendship toward the Crimean Khanate. This was made easier for him by the enmity of his enemies, the Poles and the Horde, toward Crimea. In his relations with the khanates, Ivan had to think first of Muscovite trade routes to the Black and Caspian seas which the khanates controlled.

When in 1475 the Turks demanded that the Crimean region become vassal to them and seized Mengli-Girei and took him to Constantinople, the Golden Horde established itself in the

Crimea. On his return Mengli-Girei had to fight for his throne against the Horde and his brothers. This brought him into closer contact with his ally, Ivan, who aided him to regain his power. The result had greater implications than a mere mutual assistance pact. With a friendly Crimea blocking Poland, the Novgorod question settled, and Kazan contained, Ivan was now able to challenge the Horde's domination. In a sense Mengli-Girei liberated Russia from the remnants of the Tatar yoke, for it was friendship with the Crimea that enboldened Ivan to resist all demands of the Golden Horde, and that, in turn, led inexorably to the defeat of the Horde. In 1500 the Horde made its last attempt to punish its Muscovite vassal by unsuccessfully attacking Moscow. In retaliation, Mengli-Girei (Ivan was at war in Poland) struck at the Horde in 1502 and destroyed it utterly, leaving the small Khanate of Astrakhan at the mouth of the Volga as a remnant. The common enemy of the Russians and the Crimeans was now gone. In his Polish wars Ivan had taken sovereignty over Ukrainian territories that the Crimeans were used to possessing and raiding, Ivan and his Crimean allies therefore fell out. With the Golden Horde gone and Kazan reduced to a Muscovite vassal, the Crimea became the only competitor to Moscow in a competition for the allegiance of Tatar remnants. The only check the merging Russian state would find in its final struggle with the Tatars would come from the Crimea. For a time the Crimea would be held in check by the Turks, who were no friends to Russia but worse friends to the Crimea, for they desired to protect Turkish commercial interests in that area. The Turks were also enemies of the Poles, knowing that the Poles as Latin Catholics were preaching a crusade, under orders from Rome, against the incursions into Europe of Sultans Selim and Suleiman.

With the death of Ivan III (1505), this favorable situation began to reverse itself, for Kazan, aching to throw off Russian sovereignty, began to expel Russians. In 1506 Kazan also began to raid Russian territory in alliance with the Nogai Tatars (wandering Tatar tribes who dominated the area from the Volga to the Aral Sea and were a remnant of the troops of Nogai, a great general of the Horde in the thirteenth century who had recruited from the tribes of the Ural River region). The next year (1507) the Crimea took advantage of the renewal of war between Poland and Russia to raid the Ukraine and seize the Astrakhan area. Russia, deeply involved in Poland, resorted to negotiation and intrigue to maintain its foothold in Kazan and to thwart the Crimea. Her diplomats were busy in Constantinople seeking to put Russia's own man on the Crimean throne, while in 1519 she managed to place a puppet from Kasimov on the throne of Kazan. The men of Kazan, however, would have nothing to do with the ineffectual Khan Sheg Ali. They expelled him and replaced him with a brother of the khan of Crimea and in union with their brothers of Crimea, Astrakhan, and the Nogai, warred on Russia. Had the Poles joined this league, Russia would have been ruined, but the Turks forced the Poles to remain out of it. It was, however, too much to expect unified action among Tatars.

When the men of Astrakhan, excited by the prospect of spoils, devastated the lands of their Crimean allies, the Crimeans withdrew from the league and Russia averted a mortal danger. Russia could not send a punitive expedition of peasant infantry against the mobile cavalry of the Crimea, so Russia made a Crimean peace without indemnity and recrimination that managed to strike at one enemy—Astrakhan—by recognizing Crimean sovereignty over that area. As fortunate as Russia seemed to have been in escaping the disaster of a total Tatar war she could not have won, the peace she made was unstable. The mere fact that the Crimean Tatars held dominion over the Astrakhan Tatars and were again (in 1523) reaching for a union with the Tatars of Kazan held within it omens of the restoration of a powerful single state. Had there again emerged a union of Kazan with the Crimea, everything that Ivan III had achieved would have disappeared. But lesser Tatar chiefs quarreled with the khan of Crimea and being resentful of him, raided as far as the Isthmus of Perekop (where they were stopped by Turkish Janissaries commanded to preserve the commercial peace of the region). Moscow again was saved, in a sense, by the Tatars of Crimea.

With the Crimea involuntarily neutral and a five-year truce with Poland and Astrakhan steadily becoming weaker, Vasili III (1505–1533), grandson of Ivan III, decided to regain Kazan.

This time instead of a bold attack he approached slowly, building forts and consolidating territory as he went. Having made these preparations, he sent a large army against Kazan. Unable to take the city, his forces devastated the countryside around it and retired. Then Vasili III ordered Russian merchants to stop their trade with Kazan and to trade instead at a fair he would set up for them at Nizhni Novgorod; thus the Asiatic trade was diverted from Kazan to Moscow and the city of Kazan was enfeebled by an economic blockade. Vasili III died in 1533, leaving Russia's Tatar problems closer to solution but still unsolved. He left also an infant son, Ivan IV (1533–1584), and a young wife, Helen. Under the regency of Helen a new type of defense was evolved against the Crimean Tatars which later was to be so successfully used in Asia. To protect against raids a line of forts was moved forward. Ahead of the line of forts—mere stockades— was a line of watchtowers that surveyed the countryside. As the area around the forts and between the forts and watchtowers became settled by Russian farmers, the watchtowers were transformed into stockades and further watchtowers built in front of them. It was a system remarkably like that to be used hundreds of years later in the American west, where forts located at strategic points in Indian territory became the nucleus of settlement and as the settlers came to dominate an area, further forts were built on the frontier.

The boyars of Moscow, shocked at Helen's notorious affairs, assassinated her. From 1538 to 1546 Russia was run by a boyar oligarchy which spent so much of its time in quarreling that foreign policy suffered from neglect. Moscow's prestige declined so much that in 1546 the Crimea again became aggressive, and Astrakhan, attracted by strength, began to move closer to the Crimea.

In 1546 Ivan IV ended his minority and took the throne of Russia. This brilliant and unstable man was to continue the policy of his father, Vasili III, which meant to continue the armistice with Poland and to continue to strangle Kazan while maintaining peace with the Crimea. In 1550 he took the city of Kazan. The fort of Sviasksh was built across the river from Kazan and 60,000 Russian prisoners were liberated from captivity. The years 1550 to 1552 were the last years of Tatar domination. The Crimean Khanate invaded southern Russia in 1552. Ivan trounced them soundly, and then turned his attention to Kazan, which had taken the opportunity offered by the Crimean invasion to throw out its Russian governor and again declare its independence. This time a very powerful Russian army with artillery conducted an extraordinarily bitter siege of a Kazan to which had rallied many Tatars of the Volga region. The Russians broke into the city and sacked it but only after every house and mosque had been fought for. After the fall of Kazan for the final time, to Moscow, it took a further five years to subdue the entire khanate. By 1557, however, the entire former khanate of Kazan was under complete Russian control. The upper Volga was opened to Russia, just as three years previously the lower Volga had been opened when Astrakhan made its peace with Ivan and accepted a Russian governor and a Cossack garrison.

In 1556 Astrakhan was annexed to Moscow. It is interesting to note some of the repercussions of the capture of Astrakhan by the Russians. The news penetrated Central Asia and the Caucasus, and soon delegations from Khiva, Bokhara, Persia, Circassia, and Georgia came seeking alliance with Moscow. Great numbers of merchants came into the lower Volga area because of the connections with Moscow and the Black Sea. Even the rather unknown, faraway, and poor Khanate of Sibir sent a message of friendship and some tribute to the conqueror of Kazan and Astrakhan, who was now commander of the land routes between Asia and Russia. Ivan responded with a diplomatic message to this petty khan of Sibir, who in turn sent only part of what he had promised as tribute. Ivan then angrily demanded and got from Sibir the full amount. The water passages from the Urals to the Volga were now open from the Caspian to the White Sea. A century of negotiation and war had culminated in freeing the eastern borders of the new Russian state from the depredations of the nomads.

The Urals—Siberia

A great merchant family, the Stroganovs, was to be instrumental in opening the newly won frontier areas. A Spiridon Stroganov is mentioned in the Chronicles for his great wealth, and when Tsar Vasili II was captured by the Tatars in 1455, the

Stroganovs were the chief contributors to the ransom fund. In 1471 a Stroganov was the commissioner of Ivan II charged with settling claims in the Dvina valley. This was Lucas Stroganov, whose business interests centered in that region. The Stroganov interests were widespread, but the chief source of their wealth lay in salt. Salt was a scarce commodity in Russia and the Stroganovs had early gotten a monopoly. Their original center of production was at the salt flats of the Caspian, but when the Caspian was blocked by the Khanate of Astrakhan, their main salt manufactory was transferred to the deposits at Ustiug on the Dvina.

In 1515 Anika Stroganov, head of the family, received the Dvina salt concessions from Moscow. In order to work and protect their deposits the family was permitted to colonize their concessions and to be exempt from state controls within their emerging commercial colony spread along the river. Anika's close ties to the government stood him in good stead. In 1556 when he needed iron for his manufactories and iron was scarce in Russia, he requested and obtained a charter to look for iron in the Perm and Yugra regions. In their excursions into the Urals in search of ore, the Stroganovs became involved in the fur trade and soon became the leading traders of the region with headquarters at Solvychegodsk on the Vychegda River. Anika's sons were just as enterprising as their father. After the fall of Kazan, they sought and obtained from the tsar a charter giving them, in effect, the right to colonize the Perm region if, in return for freedom from state trade restrictions, they fortified the region for Moscow. As a result of this charter, a large proprietary colony grew on the western slopes of the Urals; it was administered by the Stroganovs as they pleased without any interference from the state. Ivan gave them this great freedom because they were not nobles but only merchants and therefore could always be controlled if such a need arose.

As a part of their duties and also to protect themselves from the various native tribes raiding out of the Urals, the Stroganovs built a series of small forts on the Ural slopes and along the Kama River. Having built these forts, they were confirmed in their seignorial rights by Moscow and further allowed to make their own weapons to arm their forts. The records cite their holdings on the Kama as being 10,500 square miles. In 1568 Jacob Stroganov received from Moscow a further grant of land on the Chusovaia River, which with the Tura and Ob was to become the main route to Siberia with Verkhoturie on the Tura River as the chief control station along the route. This 1568 grant, however, put a Russian colony within an area that did not recognize Russian rule. Ivan was, in effect, giving away non-Russian land. This colony was therefore to acquire an aggressive character although in the eyes of Moscow its nature was defensive in that its purpose was to protect the salt, iron, and fur trade from raids from Siberia and to create a barrier against the natives. For their part the native Voguls, centered at Pelym on the Tavda River, resented this incursion into their tribal hunting grounds. A mutual antagonism arose between the natives and the colonists. In 1572, this antagonism broke out into an uprising of the natives within the Kama colony that had to be quelled by an army sent from Kazan. After this, Moscow advised the Stroganovs to hire Cossacks as a defense force and also to use every effort to win the natives over by peaceful means. Neither Ivan nor the Stroganovs knew that the rebellion had been inspired by the petty khans beyond the Urals headed by the khan of Sibir. If Ivan had known it, he might not have given the Stroganovs the charter of 1574 that yielded them the lands of the Tavda and Tobol rivers which constituted a goodly share of the northern part of the Siberian Khanate.

The Siberian Khanate controlled the Tobol, Irtysh, and Ishim rivers and all waterways west of them to the Urals. It was a large territory with ill-defined boundaries, comprising both forest and steppe land. In the thirteenth century this territory had been part of that of the Golden Horde, but with the decline of the Horde it had split off as an independent khanate. It was an unstable state due to constant rivalry between leading houses. Its capital was at Tiumen and its dynasty was related to the Shebanid dynasty of Bokhara. This illustrates the interconnection of Tatar-Mongol groups throughout Asia that was to draw Russia into intimate relations with both Asian nomad and settled civilizations as it expanded. Khan Ibak of Sibir had established a relationship with Ivan III in 1489, as has been previously noted, but in 1494 Ibak was assassinated by a rival, Mahamet. Mahamet then fled to the mouth of the Irtysh River and founded there Isker (or Sibir, near modern Tobolsk). With this the Siberian Khanate split into two with Mahamet at Isker maintaining good relations with Russia, but Kulak, son of Ibak at Tiumen, raiding into Russian territory. Moscow, unaware of this division of the Siberian Khanate, naturally assumed that the Siberian Khanate was breaching its agreements made with Ivan III and that therefore it had a sufficient grievance against the Siberian Khanate. Relations changed—in 1555 the khan of Sibir called on Moscow to aid him against claims being made on him by Bokhara. Moscow sent no aid but did accept the khan's fur presents as tribute and henceforth regarded Sibir as a vassal. In 1563 the fur tribute stopped coming from Sibir. In 1569 Ivan demanded that it again be sent. It was sent in 1570, and in 1571 Sibir and Moscow exchanged ambassadors. Relations between the two states now being regularized, there seemed to be no reason for a breach of the peace between them, certainly not on the side of Russia, which was now pursuing a cautious foreign policy on all fronts.

Despite the conquest of Kazan and Astrakhan and the amity with Crimea, Sibir, and Isker, there still existed troublesome remnants of the Horde who persisted in interfering with the new growing Russian trade with Central Asia via the Volga. To protect this trade and the Russian colonies on the Volga and Caspian, it was necessary to maintain good relations with the peoples and tribes in the east. Furthermore, Russia's manpower and resources had been exhausted in a twenty-year struggle with Sweden and Poland for the territory of Livonia and access to the Baltic. Peace with Poland did not come until 1582, and peace with Sweden did not come until 1583—and for Russia it was a peace of exhaustion. At the same time the opening of the English depot at Archangel was creating a great demand for furs—a most profitable item of trade for the crown—and the success of the fur trade largely depended on the maintenance of peace in the trapping regions. This spelled a peaceful expansion eastward in order to open yet greater fur territories, and the Stroganovs were the agents of this expansion. (It cost Moscow nothing to govern the Ural colonies or to police the frontier since the Stroganovs did this; yet Moscow under its charters came in for a part of the Stroganov profits). It was precisely as these matters came together—the retreat from an aggressive western policy and the initiation of a cautious policy of expansion in the east— that Kuchum, the new khan of Sibir, began an aggressive policy of encouraging native risings to drive the Stroganovs back from his frontiers. These risings were quelled by the colonial proprietors but were followed by devastating raids into Stroganov lands. The Stroganovs asked Ivan for further concessions to enable them to stop these raids. In 1574 Ivan IV gave the Stroganovs the charter of rights and property along the Tobol River (to which he had no claim whatsoever) as well as the right to arm a force and send it on a retaliatory raid into Siberian territory. In effect, the Stroganovs were given the northern part of the Khanate of Sibir. The Stroganovs set to work slowly and carefully to build up a force. Russia was then full of German, Swedish, and Polish war veterans who were prepared to accept freebooting commissions. These men were hired, and together with some tributary natives and a group of Volga Cossacks were formed into a punitive and plundering expedition to teach the khan of Sibir a lesson. The leadership was given to the Cossack Ermak Timoshiev, who had raised the men while the Stroganovs provided the means. It was expected that Ermak would return with enough loot to cover the costs of the expedition.

The main source for the story of Ermak's raid is the Siberian Chronicle, which was written many years after the event. It consists of the Stroganov Chronicle (which is favorable to that family) and the Remezov Chronicles that were written during the second half of the seventeenth century by some amateur of geography and history who incorporated within them parts of still other records. These records provide the base for all the following information on this pivotal event.

Ermak started in 1579 with 540 Cossacks, 300 Stroganov men, three cannons, and some muskets. We know that he started along the Chusovaia River. He then went to the Serebrianka River and wintered on the western slopes of the Urals. In the spring of 1580 he crossed the Urals to the tributaries of the Taghil River. The Siberian khan had no information on this. If he had, he most certainly would have fought at the frontier and not deep within his own territory. Ermak went from the Taghil to the Tura River and plundered his way along the Tura until he reached Tiumen.

At the Tiumen, full of spoils and uncertain as to the future, he attempted to negotiate with Sibir. Taking this as weakness, Kuchum Khan determined to resist. Where the Tura flows into the Tiumen a bloody battle of several days began.

Ermak emerged victorious but badly shaken in morale. He was low in supplies, his forces had taken grievous losses, and he was a long way from friends and help, but he received word that the Tatars were just as nervous and uncertain as he was. Far from attempting to cut him off in the field and destroy him, which their position and superiority indicated they ought to do, they were preparing a desperate defense. The decisive struggle took place between the mouths of the Tavda and Irtysh rivers at Chuvashev. For five days the forces of Ermak and those of Kuchum struck at each other. By the end of the fifth day Kuchum retreated and Ermak entered the settlement of Sibir. As the local natives made their submissions to him, Ermak now made a personal decision that was to have enormous consequences in the creation of the Russian empire in Asia. His problem was this: he was an employee of the Stroganovs and he did not even have a nominal responsibility to Moscow. He had carried out his orders with a success beyond the wildest plans of the Stroganovs. His duty lay in informing his superiors of the completion of his mission and, now that his punitive expedition had ended, in retracing his steps to the west. He was desperately low on men and supplies, and the best he could do was dispatch a messenger with information and wait for supplies and relief. After occupying Sibir and receiving submissions, his ambition and imagination reached from the Stroganovs to the tsar, and he decided to send the news directly to Moscow and to request Moscow for aid. This he did, directing his agent to avoid Stroganov territory.

Back in Moscow at this time (1581), news began to filter in of armed native raids across the Urals and along the Kama River. The Stroganovs wanted help and Ivan ordered his local officials to help them. Ivan had not been informed of the Ermak expedition. When he received news from his men in the area that the raids, against which he had ordered them to give help, were the results of an aggressive Stroganov policy and also that the Stroganovs had stripped the area of its pledged defense forces in order to send them across the Urals, Ivan became furious. He instantly ordered the Stroganovs to reorganize the frontier defenses. He accused the Stroganovs of alienating the natives, of not defending the marches, and of deliberately creating trouble with the khan of Sibir. He further commanded that Ermak be recalled and hung. Shortly after the dispatch of these orders, Ermak's man arrived in Moscow with beaver, fox, and sable pelts. When Ivan found from him that Sibir was at his feet at no cost, thus compensating Moscow for its losses in the west, the tsar forgave Ermak all his crimes and sent forth a relief expedition and a governor-general for the region.

Meanwhile, Ermak had been protecting his conquest by raiding out from Tobolsk. Through sheer lack of force, he resorted to a policy of terror in order to pacify the areas of the lower Ob River and the Tavda. (This was in marked contrast to the Moscow policy of cultivating the upper classes and exercising a police control over the natives through their own rulers. The first Siberian prisoner of war, Mahmet Kui, commander of Kuchum's army, was cordially received in Moscow and given a high position in the Russian army). Even aided as he was by the civil strife among the Tatars, his forces were steadily weakening when, in 1583, further aid arrived from Moscow under the command of Prince Bolkhovskoi. The arrival of more men proved to be little help, for food was terribly short. Ermak had failed to cultivate those natives who might have provided for the Russian garrison and many of his men died of starvation in the winter of 1583–1584. Sensing this weakness, the Tatars under Karacha laid Sibir under seige. The siege was repulsed, but a relief caravan that had set out from Bokhara was delayed by Tatar attack. Now desperate for food, Ermak tried to clear the area by raiding out from his base at Sibir. On one of these raids he was attacked and drowned.

Without their leader, the remainder of the Russians, downhearted, left Sibir and went down the Irtysh River to the Ob and then to the Pechora. The Tatars occupied Sibir and continued their own internecine quarrel. A relief column under Mansurov arrived from Moscow, surveyed the situation, moved past Sibir, and built a fort at the mouth of the Irtysh. The local Ostiaks, sick of Tatar fights, voluntarily submitted to Mansurov, who gave them charters confirming them in their hereditary lands, which were placed off bounds for Russians. Mansurov returned to Russia to report, and in 1586 a third relief column was sent to Siberia. This one, however, had orders to proceed slowly and consolidate territory as they went. It was this third expedition of 1586 that established the initial Russian hold on Siberia. Tiumen was occupied, fortified, and used as a base for all further operations. Here at Tiumen the first Russian church in Siberia was built. Here at Tiumen, Cossack freebooters and streltsy (men of the first permanent Russian army organized by Ivan IV), charged with the duties of frontier police and with maintaining order in the settlements, came to settle with their families. In 1587, 500 reinforcements arrived with orders to build a fort at the mouth of the Tobol. The result was Tobolsk, which controlled traffic from the Tobol and the Irtysh into the Ob and which threatened Sibir. In 1586, Sibir was taken by treachery.

Ivan IV died in 1584. His feebleminded successor, Fedor, died in 1598. Almost from the outset of Fedor's reign, the real power was in the hands of the regent Boris Godunov. Godunov's Siberian policy was to establish forts at strategic points and then to build strongpoints near enough to native groups to prevent them from making alliances with each other. Over decades the system of rivers and portages from the Pechora to the Ob was wrested from the native Voguls and Ostiaks. By completing the conquests of Ermak and consolidating the Tobolsk area, Moscow was abandoning her defensive policy on Russia's eastern frontiers.

The new policy was an aggressive one that dominated the vital river systems of the frontier and was based on control of the portages by means of forts. By 1600 there was a fortified route from the Kama to the Irtysh. In the brief period from the expedition of Ermak to the completion of the Kama-Irtysh route, the Moscow state had created a base for the exploration, conquest, and colonization of Siberia. It had developed the basic methods of (1) an advancing frontier, (2) the absolute control of portages, and (3) a native policy of divide and rule. In organizing the beginnings of a colonial government, the Moscow state was beginning one of history's epic territorial conquests.

Part **3.**

The Moving Frontier

From the Ob to the Pacific

From Tobolsk, the cornerstone of the Russian empire in Asia, a chain of blockhouses was erected along the Ob and the Irtysh between 1595 and 1606 (when Tomsk was founded). In this decade the continued eastward direction of Russia across Siberia was set, for stiff Kirghiz and Kalmuck resistance blocked penetration to the south. Furthermore, there were greater gains to the eastward for always to the east lay furs and the fur trapping natives, while to the south the natives were horse nomads. So until 1606, Moscow consolidated the Ob region, laying a minimum fur tribute on the natives to prevent them from migrating or from resisting, and in general constructing a base of future operation. In 1598 with the death of Fedor, last of the Muscovite dynasty, Russia began her famous *Smutnoe Vremia*, or "Time of Troubles." This was to last until 1616, the year of the election of Michael Romanov as tsar. The worst period was from 1606 to 1613 and during this time the Russian hold on the Ob region was nearly lost. Russia collapsed into anarchy, class war, struggles among pretenders to the throne, foreign invasion, and civil strife. Siberia's development was not only slowed down, but the noticeable weakening of the Russian power and presence was brought to the attention of the natives. A series of uprisings ensued that, if they had been concerted, would have driven the Russians from Siberia. It was only a lack of unified action among the tribes that enabled Moscow to remain in the Ob valley.

The valley of the Ob is a plain, and the area from the Urals to the Enisei River was so like the North Russian plain that it was the easiest part of Siberia to develop and control. The northern part of the Ob valley was then inhabited by Samoyeds of obscure origin. On both sides of the Urals were the Finnish Voguls. On the middle Ob and running to the Enisei were the Finnish Ostiaks. The Ostiaks were fishers and hunters who raised reindeer and dogs for food and transportation, used bows and arrows, traded deerskins with peoples to the south of them for wool and silk, and used light boats of bark and fire-hollowed log canoes. Much more sophisticated than their northern Samoyed neighbors, they trapped and clubbed their game to avoid damage to skins. Like many Siberian tribes, they practiced slavery. The Russians who objected to and forbade the enslavement of natives by Russians did not interfere with this native system, but they did forbid another objectional Ostiak practice—that of human sacrifice. To the south of Ostiak territory lay a vast region of Turkic peoples under Mongol influence of whom the most prominent were the Kirghiz of the grasslands of the Ob, Irtysh, and Enisei tributaries. South of the Kirghiz country and on the slopes of the Sayan range were the Altyn khans. Farther to the south were the Jungarian Kalmucks. The steppes around Lake Balkash were the domain of Kalmucks, whose periphery ran all the way to the steppes south of the Urals. All of these tribes were well organized and strong in the seventeenth century and Moscow was in no position to subdue them; so until 1618 Moscow contended itself perforce with maintaining a fortified line along the Ob.

Prior to the "Time of Troubles" only small parties of "serving men" (state employees who did military service) had been sent to the isolated forts of Siberia. In the "Time of Troubles," however, rumors spread that across the Urals men could find wealth and peace. A Siberian fever of hope and acquisition grew among all elements trapped in the horrors of the civil wars of European Russia. The peasants wanted to escape the growing stranglehold of the new serfdom. Debtors wanted to get out and recoup. A wave of colonists went into Siberia. The way was terribly hard, for these people had no means, being largely uprooted peasants. The government was interested in them, for it wanted agricultural colonists to provide food for the garrisons and it desired that they settle in particular places. Since the government had no means to direct these people once they were across the Urals unless they appeared in the few government villages and forts, it could not control the influx aside from encouraging it by leaving the road to Siberia unguarded. A wave of volunteer colonists went into Siberia. In addition to these settlers there was also considerable colonization of a temporary nature sent out by businessmen who organized their own expeditions to Siberia for profit. These were company groups which had managers and carried trade goods to hire trappers and pay for furs.

In addition to the peasants and the businessmen, representatives of the Orthodox church came to the Ob. In the seventeenth century alone, about fifteen monasteries were built in Siberia. These were not centers of contemplation but asylums for the old and centers of medical care, spiritual help, relief, and welfare.

In 1618, after the end of the "Time of Troubles" and under the new Romanov dynasty, a veritable explosion of explorations began that by 1639 carried Russian frontiersmen to the shores of the Pacific. The rivalry of the towns of Tomsk and Mangazeia in the exploitation of the Enisei system led to the founding of Eniseisk (1619), which became the base of exploration of the region and an administrative center equal with Tomsk and Tobolsk. From Eniseisk and its satellite town, Krasniorsk, on the upper Enisei, parties pushing through the Tunguska rivers came into the sources of the Lena and went down the Lena itself in 1630. Yakutsk was founded on the Lena in 1631 and it became the base for expeditions moving north and east. In 1636 Tomsk fitted out an expedition under Kopylov that was designed to explore the Lena. Members of Kopylov's party became the first Europeans to stand on the northeastern edge of Asia when in 1639 they reached the Sea of Okhotsk. In fifty-five years Russia had crossed Siberia; this pioneering epic is history's most stunning example of a moving frontier.

The Settlement of Western Siberia

While the drive across the land was going on, a working administration for Siberia was being set up back in Moscow. The administration of Siberia, until the later reforms of the eighteenth century, was in the hands of the Siberian Office (*prikaz*) (until 1637 the Kazan Office). The prikaz system of administration went back for centuries, originating in the household offices of the various Kievan princes. With the emergence of Moscow, the household bureaus of the grand duke of Moscow became charged with such far-reaching matters as finance, war, and foreign relations. There offices once charged only with regulating the domain and retinue of the lord, now were bureaus of state administration. (Just as the household offices of the Frankish mayors were the seed of the royal administration of the later national state.) Each office was headed by a boyar and under him were two secretaries (*diaki*) as well as clerks (*podiachii*); thus the affairs of a prikaz were divided among several desks. Originally, Siberian affairs had been handled by the Foreign Affairs Office (*posol'skii prikaz*); then they had been transferred to the Novgorod prikaz and to the Kazan prikaz. After its conquest, Siberia got an independent prikaz all its own. There was no matter concerning Siberia, whether it was the care of furs, colonization, supply of the garrisons, native policy, or administration of justice, that did not come under the jurisdiction of the Siberian Office. Since the administration of Siberia was always military and because of the peculiar conditions inherent to the settlement and exploitation of this vast land, the office allowed the administration of Siberia to develop characteristics of its own. When it came into conflict with other offices that handled affairs impinging on Siberia, such as the Office for Foreign Affairs, the Military Office, and so on, the Siberian Office generally had its own way, for as early as 1684 the tsar decreed that responsible officials in Siberia should obey only the orders of the Siberian Office.

The men that the Russian state sent to Siberia at the top administrative level (apart from the independent traders, hunters, and adventurers who were, in the main, the real conquerors and explorers of Siberia,) were men of a new class created by Ivan IV during his vast and terrible struggle to centralize power from 1564 to 1584. During this time he had destroyed or ruined the old nobility and replaced them by the small land-owning class who held their estates and favors in return for military service to the state. These men, whose lives were necessarily devoted to the state service, became the backbone of the Siberian government, and thus there was a constant military cast to the administration. This was understandable, not only because of the training and experience of each *voevoda* (governor) but also because the wild nature of Siberia and the frequent necessary native pacifications demanded a military vigilance and ability that could not be supplied by civil administrators. These men (and this is true of the independent merchant and trapper) were hard, tough, durable, and able. Like the young men of the East India Company, they were out to make their fortune if possible, but unlike the clerks and military men of that company, they had to live off the communities they managed and defended. (Siberian salaries were hardly ever paid.) Also unlike East India Company men, they were not in the midst of a treasure house that held the accumulated wealth of milleniums of civilization. Siberia was a hard land whose wealth lay in furs, and the search for furs entailed great physical hardship and risk. The bulk of the garrisons were regular army transferred from European garrisons and settled in Siberian communities and fixed in one spot, becoming in return for lifelong military service the owners of land and businesses.

The hard work on the frontier and on patrols was done mainly by mercenaries (veterans, prisoners of war, and political prisoners) formed into a foreign legion (*Litva*) and Cossacks who settled the frontier in return for freedom and exemptions from taxes and conscription. Military service in Siberia was long and dangerous, and the military suffered from the same lack of the elementary necessities, not to say comforts, of life as did almost all Siberian settlers. Pay was short, discipline was severe, and mutinies among the garrisons were not unknown. While the ultimate power in Siberia lay in the hands of the Siberian Office (and hence with the tsar), the government entrusted reasonable powers to its voevodas on the spot. Between 1594 and 1676 five administrative districts (*razriadi*) were created, but later, in 1693, this was changed to four that were more or less groups of settlements within a large area centering around some chief town. They were Tobolskii, Tomskii, Yakutskii, and Eniseiskii. Tobolsk became the center of administration but not of a centralized administration, for the governors of every chief Siberian city reported directly to Moscow. Tobolsk acted as the mediator between the various governors and as a center of military and supply operations. Aside from this, it was only a regional center as were Tomsk, Eniseisk, and Yakutsk. Each Siberian town was governed by a voevoda and a diak, each of whom was appointed directly from Moscow. The voevoda was commander of military forces, head of civil affairs, and chief dispenser of justice. The diak shared control of civil affairs and audited the accounts. All important decisions were taken in joint responsibility by both men. Further, in each town the Orthodox church was a significant force. This was due partly to the activities of Bishop Kiprian, who arrived in Siberia in 1621 and brought order into the Siberian church, which previously had been under secular direction, and partly to the position of the Patriarch Filaret in Moscow, who, as father of Tsar Michael Romanov, was the real power in Russia.

Filaret, interested in the morals of the serving men, for there was an absence of women on the frontier, gave Kiprian support in the form of grants of land (exempt from taxes) on which the church settled peasants and gained their labor in return for offering the best conditions in Siberia. The church also acted as the "eyes of the sovereign" by keeping a check on the actions of the civil authorities. As time passed the church became overly acquisitive. Through gift, grant, usury, and outright seizure, its land holdings reached the point where it was a serious block to orderly colonization. The government, concerned over the complaints of both Russians and natives, interceded in 1678 with the decree that no one could will or donate land to the church. A decree of 1697 declared that the church in Siberia had to report its income and stop all but necessary construction activities.

The efforts of the church to regulate morality with great strictness and severity turned the Orthodox population against them. At the same time voevodas sent back complaints of ecclesiastical interference with civil and military affairs and reports on the much more serious clerical interference with the collection of fur tribute from the natives. In this latter example, the church was simply pursuing its humane obligations toward the natives by acting as a buffer between the natives and the Russians. Any baptized native was treated as a Russian citizen, thereby releasing him from the payment of tribute. The reader is again reminded that the basis for the conquest and exploration of Siberia was its wealth in furs, and this depended upon a Russian policy toward the natives that ensured an uninterrupted flow. In every sense, native policy was the key to the economic success or failure of the Siberian enterprise. The natives of the tundra, taiga, and river valleys of Siberia were backward, disorganized, and ill-armed. The Russians, however, were such a small minority in such a vast land that to hold territory and its potential wealth, a fundamental policy of reconciliation was adopted. As has been noted, the initial step in new territory was to dominate the waterways of a tribal area by forts and to divide the natives. Any attempt of the natives to unite for action was nipped by fomenting intertribal hostility. Then the tribal area became a tribute area. The native chiefs and upper classes were granted favors and rank and, in effect, became Russian agents and officials. In some cases, they were granted patents of nobility (although this was far more common with the steppe people than with the northern natives). In this policy of conciliation, native customs and religion were left untouched. Religion was a thorny problem. Women were short in Siberia and baptized native women could marry serving men. On the other hand, a baptized native was free of the obligation to pay tribute. Since the government placed a greater value on furs than on the domestic bliss of its male settlers, the clergy was severely restricted in conversions. By order of the tsar, Russians were not to harm natives or penetrate native hunting reservations. Once a tribe had taken an oath of loyalty to the tsar, remained pacific, and delivered its tribute, they were regarded as friends and wards. Their complaints were honored and the voevodas were under instructions to use decent treatment. The reasonableness of this policy cannot obscure the fact that its execution was often shot through with brutality nor that the good conduct of the tribes was insured by a system of taking hostages, a practice not ended until 1769. That a humane policy made in Moscow was often inhumanely executed in Siberia by hard pressed officials in a hard pressed land was due not only to the caliber of the executants but to the fact that a clement native policy contradicted the instructions to Siberia to seek as much profit as possible for the sovereign. This meant the forcible extraction of furs from natives by local officials, and the results were the refusal to pay tribute, raids on isolated forts, and even suicide.

The most common method of native resistance, however, was

to run away and cross the Russian frontiers. The great need for food in Siberia led to one attempt to turn the natives into farmers. This was done in Tobolsk in the 1620s but was not successful. The government also encouraged its employees to farm by grants of land. (The public lands in Siberia were never sold but willingly granted to prospective farmers.) The bulk of the grain that fed Siberia was obtained from peasant immigrants who came to the land of free land and free men. Not that all came voluntarily—for aside from volunteer recruitment, the state filled its needs by ordering districts in European Russia to fill quotas for immigration. This was not as bad as it sounds, for once in Siberia a peasant, whether quota or volunteer, received land and tax exemptions. In return, the peasant cultivated a plot of state land in addition to his own. Tenure was freehold, and this alone stimulated farming in Siberia despite the interference of local officials with their demands for corvee and excess grain deliveries. By the last quarter of the seventeenth century, Western Siberia could not only feed itself but supply grain to Eastern Siberia. The peasant villages of Siberia were under a petty area official, who in matters of taxes and justice represented the government, but each peasant community itself was under a free farmer (slobdchik) who had started the village and into whose charge the government committed it after it was organized.

To the voevodas, diaks, and priests there was added one further element of government. Moscow, which was drawing wealth in fur tribute from Siberia, wanted to make sure that it was getting prime pelts and not being cheated either by private merchants or by its own officials. Therefore, an independent custom administration was set up. Customhouses were set up at all important points and all trade to and from Siberia was channeled (after 1619) through Verkhoturie and Berezov. At the customhouses a tax was placed on all goods coming into Siberia and a tax was placed on all furs in private hands that came out of Siberia. Further, to insure that the best furs were turned over to the government, private merchants were forbidden to trade with the natives until the annual fur tribute had been collected; otherwise the natives would have saved their best furs for the higher private exchange rate. The fur tribute (iasak) was the mainstay of the Siberian (and for a long time the Muscovite) finances. The exaction of a tribute was not something the Russians concocted, for it was as old as Tatar rule in Asia. The Russians merely regularized it. They collected either from the tribal chief as a feudal due, as an assessment on the whole tribe, or, most commonly, as an individual assessment wherein each native was assigned an annual quote of furs. At the end of the hunting season collections were made at designated points. The furs left over after the collection of iasak (and official extortion) could be sold either to government agents or private merchants. The government also collected property and poll taxes in Siberia and went into business in competition with private merchants by monopolizing whiskey, salt, tobacco, gold, and silver. While the revenue drawn from Siberia was large, the expenditures allowed were scanty and the whole Siberian enterprise was kept on short rations, for the Russian state desperately needed money and what it got from Siberia it spent elsewhere. The Siberian fur revenue alone not only covered the cost of the administration of Siberia but furnished, in addition, probably almost a quarter of the total revenue of Russia.

So important were the customs and other revenues of Siberia that the customs service was taken out of the hands of the voevodas in 1646. It was placed directly under financial agents of the Siberian Office. Businessmen in the various Siberian communities, men with no connection to the state except an oath and who were selected by the other businessmen of their community, were then empowered by the office to act as financial censors over the voevodas and diaks, to audit the books, check the deficits, and supervise the collection of furs. In nowise was Moscow disposed to greatly trust men in power at great distances, and in every situation a system of mutual checks was instituted. The policy of divide and rule used with the natives was equally employed by Moscow toward its own servants in Siberia.

Kolyma–Indigirka–Anadyr

Northeast Siberia is a barren land of permafrost and the men who traversed it lacked the most elementary comforts. Cold, inhospitable, dangerous, it was a land God forgot; yet men pressed on, spending years on the tundra or the ice packs. In 1636 Elisei Buza, leading a party of ten military men and forty *promyshlen-*

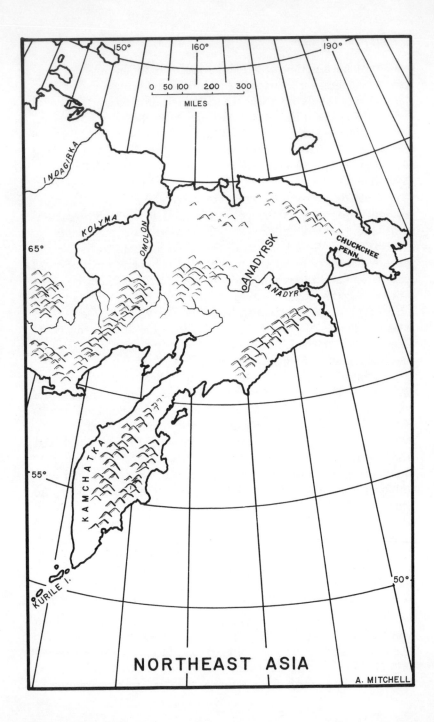

150°   160°   190°

0 50 100   200   300

MILES

INDAGIRKA

KOLYMA

OMOLON

65°

ANADYRSK

ANADYR

CHUCKCHEE PENN.

KAMCHATKA

55°

KURILE I.

50°

NORTHEAST ASIA

A. MITCHELL

niks or frontiersmen, left Eniseisk to go down the Lena to the Arctic Ocean. On the ocean edge he turned west to the next river (Olensk) and went up that as far as he could go and then returned overland to Eniseisk. He repeated this, but the second time he turned east on the Arctic coast to the next river (Yana) and returned to Eniseisk along that. In 1638 Ivanov Postnik crossed the mountains to the Yana River, went through Yakut country, and in 1640 reached the Indigirka River. He settled on the Indigirka and with the indefatigable energy and optimism of the frontiersmen, began the subjugation of the local Yukaghir.

He reported back that it was practicable to build a fort on the Indigirka and the merchant Vasili Piorkov of Eniseisk financed another expedition into the Indigirka country under Zyrian and Dezhnev. This outfit helped complete the conquest of the Indigirka and then moved east to the Alazeia River to levy iasak. Attracted by and desiring to share in this new wealth, the voevoda of Iakutsk dispatched Michailo Stadukhin by sea in 1643 to the mouth of the Lena. Here Stadukhin built open boats of galley type driven by oars and coasted eastward along the Arctic rim. Poor sailors in poor ships, his company was able to sail only in the summer, but they coasted as far as the mouth of the Kolyma River and went up that river and built a stockade on its middle course. These remarkable expeditions, handsful of men in a vast and unknown land, were universally able to enforce their will on the natives and to exact fur tribute because of a complete lack of organization among the primitives they encountered. It was in 1648 that a group led by Semen Dezhnev reached the Anadyr mouth by coasting from the mouth of the Kolyma. From the Anadyr, this party began the most remarkable small boat voyage in maritime history, traveling by sea from the Anadyr in what were little more than large rowboats around East Cape, through what was later called Bering Strait to the Pacific Ocean, and landing south of the Anadyr Peninsula. Those who survived traveled overland for three months on their return to the Anadyr River post and once there proceeded with the work of subjugation and the collection of tribute. The latter task was made difficult by the fact that on his return Dezhnev had met Stadukhin at Anadyr and the two men had quarreled, neither wanting to relinquish to the other any of the glory for exploration of the region. The natives, having now witnessed Russians fighting each other, refused to cooperate. However, the Russians used the time-honored method of holding hostages to ensure the payment of iasak and by the seventeenth century's midpoint, the Anadyr region was well known and settled.

Buryat—Baikalia

The first contacts of Russians with the formidable Buryat Mongols of the Lake Baikal region came in the form of clashes on the upper Enisei in the 1630s. An expedition of 1627, out to verify the legend of silver mines in Buryat country, was stopped by native attack and turned back. In 1628, Peter Beketov left Eniseisk and got as far as the sources of the Upper Tunguska. In 1629, Yakov Khripunov, voevoda of Eniseisk, ascended the Upper Tunguska to the Ilim River, went up the Ilim to the headwaters of the Lena River, crossed to the Angara River, and went down that river to Lake Baikal. At the portage between the Ilim and the sources of the Lena, he built a fort. This was Buryat territory and while the Buryats were tough and formed large communities, the Russians had two advantages. First they had secured the Lena River approaches to Baikal. Second, Buryat organization suffered from that fatal defect of all the Siberians vis-à-vis the Russians—they were unable to organize against Russian encroachment. Russian atrocities turned the Buryats to hostilities and in 1635 they stormed Bratsk and massacred the garrison, bringing on themselves a series of reprisals. These forced them to move to the east and returned Bratsk to Russian hands, although the Baikal area was not really secure until Irkutsk was built in 1652. The garrisons at Bratsk, Ilimsk, Irkutsk, Balagansk, and Barguzin, which controlled the routes to Baikal, were among the most refractory in Siberia. Difficult to control, their notorious actions against the natives spurred on local uprisings. Often when these were put down and the garrisons punished for their deeds, they would mutiny against their punishment. Some would desert and strike out to the east where, it was said, there were riches along the rivers called Selenga and Shilka. In 1646, an official party under Pokhatov ascended the Selenga and reached Urga, the capital of Mongolia, and persuaded the Mongols to send ambassadors to Moscow. In 1654 Beketov reached the

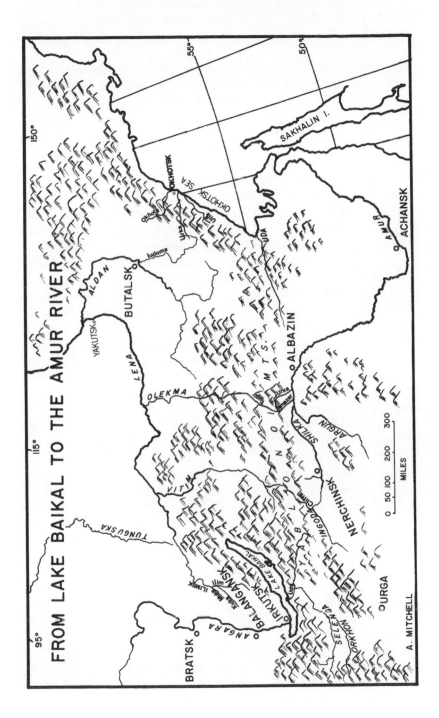

FROM LAKE BAIKAL TO THE AMUR RIVER

Shilka and built a fort at the mouth of the Nercha just where it comes into the Shilka. This fort he called Nerchinsk. With Nerchinsk the story of the Amur region begins.

Amuria

The first news of the Amur region began to get back to Yakutsk in the late 1630s. The information was generally to the effect that the land was fertile, which was true, and that silver could be had there, which was not true. Both items interested Yakutsk for it was short of both food and money and the voevoda was determined to reach this Amur land. The first Russian group to reach the Amur was that of 1643–1646 under Vasili Poiarkov.

This group went up the Aldan River to its tributaries, crossed the tributaries to the Yablonoi range, struggled across that formidable barrier to the Zeia River, and went down the Zeia to the Amur. Banking on the stories of the fertility of the Amur region, Poiarkov carried only enough food to reach that river. In view of the unknown, he preferred to carry a great weight of ammunition instead of food. The Yablonoi Mountains were crossed during the winter and one-third of the party was left to winter in the mountains and to bring along heavy supplies the following spring.

Past the mountains and on the Zeia River, Poiarkov met with his first disappointment when the natives told him there were no precious metals along the Amur and that all of the cloth and metal that they used came from trade with a people farther to the south of that great river. Seventy men accompanied Poiarkov down the Zeia to the large native town of Moldikichid, reputedly a wealthy center. The inhabitants were most friendly. The Russians, mistaking this for weakness, demanded entrance to the town, which was fortified. When the Russians threatened to torture the hostages they had taken, the town rose and put the Yakutsk party to rout. By this time the winter had fallen, Poiarkov had exhausted his provisions, and the natives of the entire region, aroused by the Moldikichid incident, refused to supply him. The winter of 1643–1644 was one of hunger so severe it even led to cannibalism. Half the force starved to death. In the spring the men left behind caught up with Poiarkov, bringing him food and ammunition. Reinforced, the Russians went down the Zeia by boat to the Amur and fought their way down the Amur to the mouth of the Ussuri where they wintered. In the spring of 1645, realizing the impossibility of retracing his steps, Poiarkov continued down the Amur to the sea, sailed north to Okhotsk, and returned overland to Yakutsk. To the voevoda of Yakutsk he submitted furs and a plan for the conquest of Amuria.

It was, however, a private merchant who brought about the penetration of the Amur valley. Erofei Khabarov was not in the service of the tsar but was a trader who, after making a fortune in salt in European Russia, had become a promoter of colonies in Siberia. Seeing the Amur as a great chance for a fortune, he told the voevoda he would undertake the costs of an entire expedition in return for official sanction. The voevoda accepted. Khabarov's instructions were simple—to arm volunteers, to proceed to the Shilka region and stop the unofficial exploitation of that region by scattered groups of Russians, and then proceed against the hostile chiefs of the Amur.

Khabarov came into the Amur valley in January of 1650. The first native villages he approached were deserted. Puzzled by this, he finally found out from hunting tribesmen that he had been preceded by Russian freebooters who had spread word that a Russian army was on its way to plunder and destroy. More importantly, he discovered that the natives of the Amur, far from being independent tribes, were paying tribute to China. Leaving a garrison behind, he returned to Yakutsk to report. He was enthusiastic about the Amur area as an answer to the overriding problem of food in Eastern Siberia. By the middle of the seventeenth century the agricultural colonies of Western Siberia could feed themselves but the colonies of Eastern Siberia were dependent on food brought with great expense and difficulty all the way from the Ob. Khabarov also thought that the Amur was rich fur territory but he cautioned that any conquest would require many men and be a difficult and dangerous feat. On his return, the expedition set off down the Amur, finding to their chagrin that the villages which had been deserted on their previous trip were now occupied and heavily fortified. Finally, at the great bend of the Amur downstream from the mouth of the Urka River, they stormed a fort garrisoned by fifty Manchus, settled a garrison in it, named it Albazin, and continued their way down

the river. Their progress was a continual running fight and in the
fall they returned to Albazin for the winter of 1651. Khabarov
sent back to Yakutsk for men and supplies, and recommendations went along for immediate agricultural colonization. Meanwhile, a series of reports on the possibilities of the Amur had
traversed Siberia to Moscow. The reports were so promising that
the decision was taken to form an army of 3,000 men under
Prince Lobanov-Rostovsky to take and hold the Amur valley.

In the spring of 1651 Khabarov left Albazin and fought his
way along the Amur to the Sungari. The resistance there was so
fierce that he stopped and established a fort at Achansk. Khabarov was now operating in territory tributary to the Manchu
dynasty of China, and in March 1652, he was besieged by a
Manchu army of 2,000 men armed with cannon and muskets.
The garrison defeated the army and seized its cannon but being
in an untenable position retreated, passing large groups of Manchus on the river bank. On the upper Amur, Khabarov met the
reinforcements that had set out from Yakutsk the previous year.
It was decided, in view of the information gained from prisoners that a large Chinese army was expected on the Amur,
to build and defend a fort at the mouth of the Zeia. At this point
Khabarov's men mutinied against him. Now he did not dare remain in the Amur; by this time the entire region was up in arms
against the Russians. Reporting his plight to Yakutsk, Khaborov
decided to winter along the Zeia.

In the years of Khabarov's explorations, the news had spread
around Siberia of this "Eldorado" of the East. A tremendous
"Amur fever" seized men and even whole garrisons deserted to
take part in the new bonanza of the Amur. As if the presence of
a swarm of deserters and fortune-seekers was not burden enough
for the harassed Khabarov, Dmitri Simoviev arrived in the Amur
to represent the government and to prepare for the arrival of
Lobanov-Rostovsky and his force. Simoviev returned to Yakutsk,
taking Khabarov with him and leaving Onofrei Stepanov as commander with orders to build three new forts, prepare 90,000
tons of corn, and send his furs directly to Moscow, bypassing
Yakutsk.

The demand for such an enormous quantity of corn was an
impossible one in an area ruined and deserted by war. The situa-

tion of the Russian party became graver and graver, and, because the fur tribute now went directly to Moscow, Yakutsk refused to cooperate with Stepanov and he was left on his own. In 1654 Stepanov was attacked at the fort of Kumarsk on the Zeia by a frontier force of the Manchu Empire. He beat off the attack and asked Yakutsk for permission to abandon the region, but he was refused. He ran so short of food in 1658 that he was forced to raid down the Sungari to collect grain. He was killed there and the remainder of his men retreated to Nerchinsk, abandoning the rest of the Amur valley. When the news of the successive catastrophes in the Amur reached Moscow, the government decided to abandon any conquest of the lower Amur River and to use Nerchinsk as the Russian advance post in the Amur area. While the government withdrew to the upper river, the lower still remained the haunt of Cossacks, freebooters, and deserters. They restored the fort of Albazin, made it a sort of free republic (it became known as the "thieves fort"), and scrupulously sent fur tribute to Moscow in order to earn amnesty. They were so successful that in 1672 Moscow took Albazin under its protection and revived its interest in the lower Amur. In 1683, however, the vigorous Manchu dynasty sent them a message at Albazin demanding that they clear out of the Amur. The garrison refused, and what till now had been a frontier incident became a war between Russia and China. A Manchu force laid seige to Albazin in 1685 while its Mongol allies advanced on the Amur along the Selenga River and also attacked the trans-Baikal region, imperiling all Russian positions between the Amur and Baikal. It was this later action that forced Moscow to come to terms with China. The Manchus allowed the Albazin garrison to withdraw with honor.

Later that year a small Russian force returned to harvest the grain crop that the Chinese had not destroyed and decided, on the spot, to rebuild and reoccupy Albazin. The Chinese returned and began the second siege of Albazin in July 1686. The garrison desperately resisted for five months and was on the verge of defeat when the Chinese retired on orders from Peking, for in October 1686, Russian representatives had arrived in Peking with a request from Moscow that all differences between Russia and China be negotiated and that pending this, Albazin be left alone.

Russia and China in the Seventeenth Century

The consequent Treaty of Nerchinsk (1689) with its important effects on Russian expansion and on Russo-Chinese relations was the result of far more than the frictions that arose between the Manchu tributaries on the Amur and the free Cossack colonists of the upper Amur. It was a manifestation of an extraordinarily complex relationship between Russia, China, and the various tribal peoples who spanned Eurasia as unstable remnants of the old Mongol Empire. To unravel this relationship and to understand how Russia and China came willy-nilly into a frontier relationship, it is necessary to turn our attention back to European Russia. In the black soil belt running south of the Urals from the lower Volga to the upper Irtysh, Moscow still had only a tenuous hold and her settlers were in constant danger from nomad raids.

This region was a frontier in flux, with Cossacks settling and patrolling the marches in return for grants of land and guarantees of personal freedom. Following the Cossacks were colonists eager to settle the rich valleys of the lower Volga, Ural, upper Ob, Tobol, and Irtysh rivers. Cossacks and peasants constantly pushed against the natives and the natives pushed back. This region was generally called Bashkiria. The Bashkirs, a Turkic people, had originally been Mongol vassals and then, with the disruption of that empire, had drifted into vassalage to the Khanate of Kazan and occupied the slopes and confines of Uralia.

After the Russian conquest of Kazan, Moscow was largely occupied with the pacification of the Bashkirs, and when peace was finally made (1556), the Bashkirs became tributary to Moscow. Despite this arrangement, Russian authority over this unruly people was never thorough and local control over them was only had by locating strategic garrisons among them. The first fort in Bashkiria and the center of Russian administration for the area was built at Ufa (1572). Despite this and other garrisons (Tara, Kuzivetsky, Ketak, Narzm, Tomsk, Makov), the Bashkirs remained a constant source of trouble. They objected to the seizure of their grazing lands for farms and towns, to the graft of the voevodas, and to the substitution of Russian law for their own customs and mores. They revolted between 1660 and 1680, spurred on by Moslem propaganda (the Bashkirs were devout

Moslems) that played on their memories of the old Moslem Mongol domination of Russia. These troubles in turn affected other tribal federations connected with the Bashkirs and dominating territory from the headwaters of the Ob to the Kirghiz (Kazak) steppe between the Caspian and the Aral seas.

One such group was the old Nogai federation now dispersed over the steppe; another was the Uzbeks (a remnant of the Golden Horde that was to the north and east of the Aral Sea on the plains south of the Irtysh); and a third was the Kirghiz of Northern Turkestan who dominated the area south of the headwaters of the Ob. The Uzbeks moved south into Turkestan, but the other two federations remained as a thorn in Moscow's side.

The Kirghiz were especially troublesome. They were a large group and originally were a confederation of tribes who had broken off from the Golden Horde and lived by raiding the Russian frontiers. They were the original "Kazaks" or freebooters. At the end of the sixteenth century their khan, moved by a desire for spoils, warred against Bokhara, the great depot in the Asian-European trade. He was defeated, but in the process the Kirghiz took over part of Turkestan. In their new territories they split into three separate groups, the Great Horde, the Middle Horde, and the Small Horde. (This tribal fluidity was a constant headache to Moscow, since it was never quite sure with whom it was dealing or whether those with whom it dealt would remain in the same place.) Since Russia placed great store on the trade out of Asia that passed through this tribal region, Tobolsk received orders to deal with the southern frontier and to protect the trade. As a result, a number of forts were built as the base of Russian expansion and control southward from the Ob to Central Asia.

Moscow was not only interested in the Asian trade but had plans to connect up further routes from Moscow to India and China and Central Asia like the valuable route from Tobolsk to Bokhara. The nomads were astride the projected routes. In addition, the Western Siberian farmers, as the single source of food for Siberia, needed protection as did valuable salt lakes on the headwaters of the Irtysh. This struggle on the rim of Turkestan brought on by the Bashkir-Kirghiz raids led Moscow into a closer relation with the powerful and terrible Kalmucks of Jungaria.

Near the end of the sixteenth century there were two powerful Mongol confederations in Mongolia proper. The Khalka Mongols of Northern Mongolia, sometimes called the Eastern Mongols, lived between the Kerulen River and the Kobdo lakes. The Western Mongols, or Eleuths, based on the Altai range, lived between the Kobdo lakes and the Tien Shan range. The Kalmucks (or Oirats or Sungars or Jungars) were a particularly fierce and turbulent component of the Western Mongols. The Eastern and Western Mongols were continually hostile to one another. By the end of the sixteenth century (1552), the Western group was slowly pressed out of its territory by the Khalkas (better known as the Altyn Khans because of their chief, the Altyn Khan or Golden Khan) and broke into four tribal groups. The Kalmuck element traveled through the Ili passes into Kirghiz country and pushed the Kirghiz into the Enisei plain.

The Kalmucks settled in Jungaria, but having no fixed frontiers and shifting to wherever plunder was available, they gradually spread from the Ili to the Irtysh, coming into contact with Russians on the sources of the Irtysh around 1606. The relatives of Kiching, khan of Sibir, found refuge with the Torgut branch of the Kalmucks, who had drifted into Volga country, which gave the Kalmucks a good excuse to claim Sibir. We have seen that the Golden Horde eventually broke into the three lesser khanates of Crimea, Kazan, and Astrakhan, but preceding and accompanying this, there was a great dispersion of Tatars from the Volga to the Enisei and from the Urals to Turkestan. Some coalesced as khanates such as the Khanate of Sibir, but for the most part they remained amorphous confederations of nomads roaming large ill-defined stretches of territory. Pressing toward Tobolsk and Tara they came into continual armed conflict with the Russians, and a situation arose where the headwaters of the Ob and Enisei came under mixed Russian-Kalmuck occupation despite the prior Russian conquest. In 1615, due to pressure from their bitter and powerful enemies, the Altyn Khans, the Kalmucks entered into friendly relations with the Russians. This lasted only for a few years however, and the Kalmucks resumed their raids into Siberian territory. Then in 1635, under a strong leader, Baatur, they entered into a formal relationship with Moscow, returning prisoners and sending a present of 1,000 horses to the tsar. Moscow accepted this eagerly as a step toward pacification of the frontiers and although for fifteen years relations were comparatively peaceful, it became obvious that Baatur could not completely discipline his people. In 1649 an unsanctioned Kalmuck raid on Tomsk resulted in breaking off relations for a decade. Baatur died in 1660. His son Galdan, who was one of the most capable leaders Asia produced, brought the tribes to heel.

Galdan had been destined to become a lama and was not trained for the Kalmuck throne. But the murder of his brother, who had succeeded Baatur, placed him in the leadership of his people. He was released from his vows and returned to his people where he pronounced himself the protector of Lamaism and defender of Islam. He was one of those rare and extraordinary nomad chiefs whose advent was always a source of worry to the Chinese empire. By ability and personality, such men were able to weld the scattered tribes of China's inner Asian frontier into a unified, formidable fighting machine and to put together one of those short-lived conquest empires which were the scourge of China. The Emperor K'ang Hsi viewed this man as a grave and fierce enemy, for Galdan swept through Moslem Central Asia and by the 1670s was in control of Sinkiang. From his capital at Kuldja he carried war to the east and the south. At this time, a civil war broke out among the Khalkas of Mongolia. Galdan took sides, invaded Mongolia, defeated his enemies in 1688, drove the Khalkas to the shadow of the Great Wall and into the arms of K'ang Hsi, and placed his forces on the Russo-Mongol borders. The Chinese, pleased by this, for it seemed to them to wall them off from the Russians as well as permit them to operate in Galdan's rear, began a vigorous colonial campaign whose prize was Mongolia. Galdan sent to Yakutsk seeking a Russian alliance in memory of the old one between Baatur and Moscow.

This request placed Russia in a difficult position. They had blundered into the great Manchu-Mongol struggle whose prize was control of the outer Mongolian steppe. Their policy in this region had been to cultivate friendship with the Altyn khans. An alliance with Galdan would mean a reversal of this policy. On the other hand it would be desirable to have a strong ally against China as well as peace on their southern flank. So Yakutsk car-

ried on a prolonged evasive policy that enabled Russia to tempo-
rize with both Galdan and the Altyn khans. The Altyn khans,
not getting the help expected from the Russians, turned to
China. Chinese agents gave them immediate support, which
meant they could use the Altyn khans against the Russians in the
forthcoming negotiations at Nerchinsk. Galdan made one final
request of Moscow for 3,000 men and artillery and promised to
ravage China to the Great Wall. Moscow was dilatory, and the
Altyn khans with Chinese help pushed the Kalmucks back to
Jungaria. This wishy-washy diplomacy hurt Russia at Nerchinsk,
but the failure to help Galdan convinced Peking of the essentially peaceful interests of Russia. This was correct, for Russia's
sole intent toward China was commercial. The first embassy
to China sent by the Treasury Office in 1653, under the command of Theodore Baikov, had gone from Tobolsk to Peking via
Jungaria and had done excellent business in Peking, although on
the return it was plundered by the Kalmucks. In 1668 another
caravan cleared 18,000 rubles on an investment of 4,500. This
kind of profit raised high hopes in Moscow about the Chinese
trade and also influenced Russian policy towards Jungaria. In
1690 Galdan entered his last struggle with China. He got within
thirty miles of Peking, but, weakened by internecine struggle, he
was routed from China and Mongolia in 1696. While Jungaria
still remained a strong state, China was now undisputed master
of Outer Mongolia.

The defeat of Galdan had an incidental effect in freeing the
upper Enisei of nomad pressures. The Kirghiz, who were pressed
between the Kalmucks and the Russians in the upper Enisei valley, had turned to Galdan for protection. Galdan's successes and
the fact that the Kirghiz had a strong leader in Irenak made the
last quarter of the seventeenth century one of perpetual warfare
on the Enisei. With the decline of Galdan, however, the power
of the Kirghiz also declined and with the death of Irenak, they
submitted to Russia, thus pacifying another stretch of the frontier. The last great tribal group of the frontier, the Altyn khans
of the Sayan range, were cultivated by the Russians, who wanted
their neutrality on the frontier or, if possible, their help against
other nomads, and a peace was effected between the two. There-

fore, near the end of the seventeenth century, Russia and China
alone faced each other across the long Mongolian-Manchurian
frontier. The prize at issue was the Amur valley, which was a
sort of no-man's-land; and this prize was to be won by negotiation and not by the war.

Russia's relations with China begin in 1653 and not in 1567 as
has generally been claimed. The earlier date is based on Chinese
chronicles but is not found in Russian accounts. The standard account is that in 1567, a Russian, Ivan Petrov, visited China and
wrote a description of his travels. Actually, this account is a confusion of later travels. The authentic records show that in 1616
Ivan Petrov went to Mongolia and not China. Petrov's account
compares Mongol farming with Cossack farming at Tobolsk,
which was not founded until 1587, and it also mentions the Patri-
archate, which was not established until twenty-two years after
the supposed date of 1567. It was Baikov's trip of 1653, followed
by the profitable embassy of 1668, that really got Moscow interested in China as a market for the growing surplus of Siberian furs. It was the Cossack Republic of Albazin that brought
China's attention forcibly to Russia in Siberia, and it was the de-
sertion to Russia of the Tungus Prince Gantimur that brought
Chinese agents into Russian territory. Gantimur went over to
the Russians at Nerchinsk in 1667. China, fearful of losing this
powerful leader who had a strong hold over the Tungus of Manchuria, sent agents into the Nerchinsk area from 1669 to 1670 to
try to get Gantimur to return. The Russians, for their part, could
not yield Gantimur, for not only had he been converted to ortho-
doxy and granted a patent of nobility but to return him would
jeopardize their policy of granting protection to the tribes from
the rapacity of Peking in return for allegiance and iasak.

The Chinese contacted the voevoda of Nerchinsk, at which
a vague frontier trade had been carried out, and as a result,
Danilo Archinski, the voevoda, sent an envoy to Peking in 1671
with the startling proposition that China become a vassal of the
tsar. The envoy saved his head by using it and did not deliver
this message. He was well received in Peking because the officials
now realized that there was a difference between official Russia
in the Amur and the freebooters. They wanted to establish just

what part of the frontier was under official Russian control and what part was under the Cossacks. When in 1672 the voevoda of Nerchinsk took Albazin under his protection, this extended the Russian's outposts farther than the Chinese anticipated or thought proper.

Then in 1675, a new Russian mission to China led by the remarkable Bessarabian Greek linguist, Nicolai Spafarii, arrived in Peking. Spafarii, who was charged with learning as much as possible about China, was given alternate credentials as minister or as ambassador and was to use that which would most impress the Chinese. (Spafarii, whose credentials were in Latin, was accompanied by a Jesuit who deserted to the resident Jesuits in Peking, an important factor in the treaty of Nerchinsk.)

Spafarii's instructions were basically mercantilist (he carried with him, as a guide, the work of Krizanich, one of the first Russians who foresaw the possibilities of mercantilist theory for Russia). Aside from such matters as impressing the emperor with the titles and dignity of the tsar, requesting an exchange of envoys, settling on the proper language for negotiations, and gaining the freedom of Russian prisoners of war (at thirty rubles a head), the bulk of his instructions were concerned with establishing a free trade between Russia and China. Spafarii tried to deliver his credentials to the emperor of China in person, but this was refused and he compromised by leaving his letter on the empty throne.

When he did receive an audience with the emperor, he ran into the usual difficulties that Westerners were to have with the Chinese court. He refused to perform the *kotow*. This was waived and he had a brief audience with the emperor. He was then asked to leave and to have Russia send an ambassador who would conform to Chinese customs. Actually, the Chinese had no intention of negotiating any question with Spafarii until the frontier problems and especially the problem of Gantimur were settled. Spafarii, having no instructions on these matters, left Peking but not before he had accomplished a great deal. He had talked with Father Verbiest, a Jesuit missioner who was one of the first scholars and diplomats of China, and had come to realize that China could not take strong measures on the Amur, because the new Manchu dynasty was having internal problems. At the same time Spafarii made clear to Verbiest (who had the confidence of the Manchu court) that the troubles in the Amur valley were due to irregular forces and did not represent official Russian policy. He, in turn, received advice from the Jesuit that Albazin should be the fartherest advance of the Russians.

Now, either from conviction of Russian designs or from designs of their own, the Chinese began to prepare for war. They constructed a dockyard at Kirin to build a flotilla for the Amur. They opened a supply route along the Sungari River and they built forts on the Amur. In 1681 the voevoda of Nerchinsk received notice from China to abandon the Russians' posts on the Zeia and the mid-Amur. He refused and the result was the siege and capture of Albazin. But, as we have seen, when the Chinese withdrew, the Russians again occupied the site. The Chinese again took Albazin (1686), and this time their Mongol allies began to put pressure on Russia in the Selenga River area. Russia, unable to send troops into the Amur, instead sent envoys to Peking to request talks. The Chinese were now glad to enter into negotiations because of their troubles with Galdan. Russia was represented at Nerchinsk by Feodor Golovin, an able diplomat, whose specific instructions were to end the dispute with China, avoid all force, obtain the Amur if possible, but if that proved impossible to offer the Zeia River as the boundary. He was given absolute leeway in arriving at these goals. Golovin left Moscow in 1686, had to fight his way through the Khalka Mongols and arrived at Nerchinsk in August 1689 with a small force. The Chinese mission was headed by Prince Songotu, who was leading 3,000 Manchu troops. Songotu's basic instruction was to not yield the Amur region but if pressed to make the boundary at the Argun River. The Chinese were accompanied by the Jesuit Fathers Gerbillion and Pereyra who conducted the negotiations in Latin.

The reason for using Latin as the intermediary tongue was obscure. In 1671 minor negotiations at Nerchinsk had been ably conducted through Mongol translators. The Russians had good Buryat Mongol linguists at their command and the officials at Peking who handled Russian affairs (along with that of other barbarians) had equally able Mongol interpreters. Latinists were hard to come by on the frontier and there is no reason why the

Chinese should have abandoned a language familiar to them (Mongol) for what must have been an exotic tongue. Whenever the Russians at Nerchinsk approached the Chinese negotiators in Mongol, the Jesuits intervened on the grounds that they were the official interpreters, and whenever the Russians approached the Chinese seeking explication of the terms proposed in Latin, the Chinese were able to respond that the Jesuits had exceeded their instructions. Probably the use of the Jesuits represented the desire of their society to bring about a peaceful agreement advantageous to China. They needed to gain the goodwill of Peking, and indeed their labors at Nerchinsk were probably instrumental in eliciting the 1692 edict tolerating Christians in China. It may also have represented a commonsense attitude by Peking whereby their learned and trusted foreigners could be used to parley with the other foreigners. As a matter of fact, after the first two days of talks, the Chinese, adamant about their own terms, were only prevented from breaking off the talks by the Jesuits.

The crucial point of the entire meeting was the delimitation of the boundary. Golovin, facing a superior force and sensible of the hostility of the Buryats, was under considerable pressures to come to an agreement. The Chinese were also impatient to conclude the talks and turn their attention to the Kalmucks who were harrassing them. Golovin, whose instructions were to hold as much territory as possible, had also to remember the Russian desire for the Chinese trade. (It is doubtful whether Moscow realized the real possibilities of the Amur region. They had never done anything to develop it nor had they ever disciplined the Cossacks who had destroyed the native agriculture.) Golovin gave ground gradually, setting himself firmly to resist that Chinese proposal that would have set the borders at the Lena River.

On August 27, 1689, a brief treaty was concluded. The Treaty of Nerchinsk set the Russo-Chinese boundaries at the line of the Argun, Gorbitsa, and Shilka rivers, along the watershed of the Lena and Amur system—then along the Stanovoi range, the Yablonoi range, and hence to the Pacific. The Amur valley was closed to Russian hunters and travelers; the Russian forts were demolished and Russian residents transported back to Russian territory. A mixed tribunal was established to judge all cases of trespassing except that done by armed bands. An agreement on the extradition of fugitives was signed which was not retroactive and which therefore excluded Gantimur. The frontier was religiously observed by both sides, but far more important, a permanent peace was established between Russia and China and free trade between those countries was agreed upon. Nerchinsk was, despite its terms, a tremendous victory for Russia. She not only gained peace and trade with China, she was not only legally recognized by the great Chinese Empire as an occupant of East Asian territory, but the definition of the boundaries was, with one small exception, vague enough to permit the greatest possible freedom of action in the future. Really, the Treaty of Nerchinsk set the boundaries to only a small part of an immense area. All of the descriptions to the northeast of Nerchinsk were simply names, the land never having been mapped. The country to the southwest of Nerchinsk, that is, Trans-Baikalia, was left without delimitation. This was not planned, but represents rather a policy of ignorance whose future benefits were to accrue to Russia.

The important commerce clause of the Nerchinsk Treaty merely provided that the subjects of either nation could, when properly accredited, come and go across the frontier on their private business. There were no stipulations as to methods of trade, the number of persons to be engaged in trade, or, most important, the number of trade depots or terminals on either side of the frontier. In the period of three years following this treaty, annual caravans of Russians appeared in Peking for trade, and the Chinese, contrary to their custom, received, housed, and entertained them. Galdan was still active; it was believed in Peking that he was approaching the Russians for assistance. As part of Chinese plans for the isolation and subjugation of the Jungars, the Chinese authorities were disposed to be extraordinarily friendly to the Russians and therefore receptive to Russian trade.

Moscow for its part wished to make this trade a government monopoly and to regularize it on an annual basis. In 1692, therefore, the first Russian "ambassador" to China started on his way. This was the Dutch merchant Isbrandt Ides who traded at Archangel. He paid Moscow a substantial sum for the privilege of organizing a caravan and he was made a diplomatic agent by Peter I (1682–1725). He carried political instructions on the return of deserters and prisoners, the establishment of a Russian Church in Peking, and other matters, but his primary instruction was to regularize the trade between Moscow and Peking. Mistakes in protocol impaired Ides' visit and it was not particularly successful on the political side, but Peking agreed to the establishment of a regular caravan trade with the stipulation that it would receive one large Russian caravan every three years.

Ides did get permission to have a Russian consul in Peking during the visits of a caravan, and he left his secretary, Lawrence Lange, as a temporary consul. Lange failed to bribe the right people and this, in addition to the normal mistakes a Westerner could be expected to make in Chinese protocol, forced him to leave Peking in 1722. Lange's lack of success was fundamentally due to matters entirely outside of his competence and knowledge.

For one thing, there was the question of the control of caravan routes. Commerce with China was a monopoly of the Russian state at the end of the seventeenth century, but illicit trading ruined it. A considerable number of private caravans misrepresenting themselves as official agents made the trip (to the increasing irritation of the Chinese, who had no way of distinguishing true from false credentials) with the official connivance of local Siberian officials and to the detriment of the Moscow treasury, which had been making profits of 100 percent on its caravans.

In the period following Ides' negotiations, Moscow gradually lost its monopoly on the caravan trade with China. This was partly due to its inability to supervise the activities of every merchant on the far frontier and partly due to the change in the caravan route that put caravans under Chinese direction. The original route had been from Irkutsk to Nerchinsk and then across Manchuria to Peking. This was the route designated by Moscow and controlled (and milked) by the voevoda of Nerchinsk. While it was the longest caravan route to Peking it made sense as long as Mongolia was a Khalka-Kalmuck battleground, but when Galdan was ultimately defeated in 1696 the short route from Irkutsk to Selenginsk to Urga to Peking, which took less than half the time, became feasible. With Chinese acquiescence, Russian caravans, flaunting their own government, began to travel this route. Since this was a route across lands controlled by Peking, the Chinese could control strictly the number of men accompanying the caravan as well as enforce other regulations that had, until then, not been enforceable. This included a flat refusal to receive any caravan that did not have the legal authority of the highest Russian official in Siberia. The extraordinary willingness of Peking to accept a kind of trade with Russia which she permitted no other nation; her voluntary opening of the Mongolian route, her reception of official Russian missions, and her later dispatch of official Chinese missions to Moscow, all were a part of Peking's continuing struggle for the control of Central Asia in which Russia was often inadvertently involved and which was not settled until 1727. This struggle, as it concerns Russia, will be related in the next part under the Central Asian and Siberian policies of Peter the Great and his successors. Suffice to say that at the beginning of the eighteenth century, Russia's policies and actions in Eastern Asia were being affected by those same forces that over three centuries before had moved them eastward—the wars of the Mongol-Turkic federations of Inner Asia.

In 1708 an uprising in Bashkiria just at a crucial moment in the Russo-Swedish war forced Peter I to request help from the Kalmucks of the North Caspian area. Ayuka, khan of these Kalmucks, came to Moscow's aid, invaded Bashkiria, plundered, slaughtered, and pacified the tribes. The Chinese heard of this and since the Kalmucks of Jungaria were a thorn in their sides, tried to enlist the Kalmucks of the Caspian against the Jungarian Kalmucks. In 1714 Peking sent an embassy to Ayuka. Moscow had no objections to this but did inform Ayuka that Russia and the Jungarians were friendly for many of the south Siberian tribes under Russian protection owed some kind of a nominal allegiance to Jungaria. The Kalmuck-Chinese conference ended in failure.

Ayuka saw no profit in getting involved in the Jungarian war. This decision strained Russo-Chinese relations, the Chinese believing that Ayuka's decision was due to Russian advice. Strangely enough, the mission to Ayuka returned to Peking with some Orthodox priests in its train. This was the beginning of the Russian religious mission in China and the source of much intelligence on China. The diplomat Leon Ismailov was sent to Peking in 1719 to smooth over the troubles arising from the caravan and border incidents. He met with little success although he had an audience with the emperor. The Chinese now were concerned over the number of Mongol families crossing into Russian territory, and they believed that Russia was encouraging Chinese subjects to emigrate. Ismailov, charged with getting a permanent Russian consulate in Peking, managed to secure permission only for a temporary consul during the visit of a caravan. Russo-Chinese relations began to degenerate. Russian traders at Urga on the Sino-Mongol frontier were beaten and expelled. Then Russia gave guarantees of good behavior on the frontier, and in 1723 the Chinese emperor allowed Urga to be reopened for the Russian trade. In 1723 Moscow sent Savva Vladislavitch as envoy to Peking. He was instructed to protest the construction of Chinese forts on the upper Irtysh, to get permission for the export of precious metals from China, and to gain permission to trade by sea at Canton. Vladislavitch's great achievement was to establish a joint frontier commission. The Chinese were rather easily persuaded that the boundary ran to the sea although it was drawn somewhat farther to the south than Moscow had anticipated.

After much maneuvering, many tricks, and a number of threats on both sides, a preliminary treaty was concluded at the Bura River in 1727, followed by the main treaty which was concluded at Kiakhta in 1727 and ratified in 1728. This Treaty of Kiakhta was the basis of Russo-Chinese relations until 1857. It provided for the establishment of eternal peace between the two countries, extradition processes on matters of border crossings, and triennial caravans to consist of no more than 200 people. In addition, a Russian Orthodox mission was allowed permanent status in Peking (one of its first steps was to establish a Chinese-language school) and it was agreed that no permanent residence in Peking would be permitted to Russian businessmen (this did not work out, as they tended to stay on).

Novgorod to Kiakhta—A Retrospect

From the days of the Novgorodian penetration of the Ural fur lands to the year of the Treaty of Kiakhta, Russia had recreated herself and had sketched the outlines of the greatest land empire in history. The old Russian cities and states were slowly pieced together in the fifteenth and sixteenth centuries, The Russians suffered and survived their unwanted role as a moat defensive for Europe against the tribes of Asia, and when the great gathering of Russia was well under way in the sixteenth century trade, accident and the old harsh facts of defense turned Russia eastward. Across the Urals and from river basin to river basin, over the portages and along the great land route (Veliky Trakt), the traders, hunters, merchants, Cossacks, and explorers traveled the long and difficult road to the Pacific Ocean. Set in motion by the hunt for furs and the depredations from the steppe, the push eastward was a boon for the fur trade it furnished to the impoverished Russian state. From need and self-interest, Russia tried to run Siberia as a government-owned and managed enterprise, a massive colonial appendage.

The actual process of exploration, conquest, and settlement bears a remarkable resemblance to the American exploration, conquest, and settlement of the trans-Mississippi West. Substitute Americans for Russians, the mountain men for the promyshlenniks, the Northwest Company for Khabarov's company, Bent's Fort or Fort Laramie for Tomsk or Ufa, the Blackfeet, Sioux, and Comanche for the Kirghiz, Bashkirs, and Kalmucks.

Obviously, there were radical differences. The Great Plains and Rockies are not Northeastern Asia, but there were many parallels: the sense of freedom, the big sky, the handsful of men facing the mountains, the rivers, the plains, the intertribal hostilities so helpful to these handsful, the lack of native coordination against the intruder. Many parallels and many differences, with perhaps the greatest parallel being the spirit of advance. In Western Siberia, that is, the great basin of the Ob River, conditions of terrain and weather were so similar to those in European Russia's central and northern areas that a fairly rapid and planned development was possible. Here, under the aegis of the Muscovite state, the fort became the focal point for control of territory, the collecting center of fur tribute, the nucleus of the settlement, and the generator of still more advanced forts, which in their turn became centers for control, collection, and settlement. Once into the unknown beyond the Enisei River, the Russian frontiersmen were on their own, and the conquest of much of Siberia was the work of small bands of men operating at great distances from advanced posts. While the hope for riches was no less with them than with men in any similar situation, it was still the love of adventure that carried them on through great danger and privation.

Perhaps the greatest difference was that at the end of the trail the United States did not come face to face with a powerful and civilized empire. The advance across Siberia was also a time of learning. Long before her actual contacts with China, Russia had been learning of that country from the Mongols and indeed was the only Western country with a chance to so learn. When the contact actually occurred is of little moment. The very struggle between the Chinese Empire and the tribal confederations for control of Mongolia and Central Asia would have inexorably brought into it any country on the periphery. The first contacts between these two empires came at a time when two new dynasties were struggling to assert their authority over their own lands, the Romanovs in Russia and the Manchus in China. With authority being menaced in each case, although in differing degree, by the horse nomads of the grass steppe and uplands, the remarkable thing is that the contact should have been so easily and rapidly productive of a treaty as notable for its brevity as for its enduring pacific effect. Kiakhta marks the end of a stage on the road east from Novgorod, a stage marked by great men and names—Ob, Enisei, Lena, Amur, Indigirka, Ermak, Dehznev, Khabarov, Galdan—but yet only a stage. The road stretched on across the Aleutians to Alaska and San Francisco, then a spur through Hawaii to Canton in the south, and finally turned back on the continent to Japan, Manchuria, Korea, and Central Asia.

If Nerchinsk was a Russian triumph then Kiakhta balanced it. China's objectives were in Central Asia and not in the Northeast. By detaching Russia from the Kalmucks at Nerchinsk, China gained a great deal, and that is why she concluded a territorially disadvantageous treaty at Kiakhta. She conquered the Mongols, neutralized Russia, and by the end of the reign of Peter I in 1725, had hegemony over her inner land frontier.

Siberia in the Eighteenth and Early Nineteenth Centuries

The accession of Peter the Great in 1689 had come at a time when the revenues from Siberia began to decline, due to abuses in government and to a real lack of knowledge of Siberian resources. Peter was to relieve both the abuses and the lack. He speeded up the doing of business, abolished the Siberian Office, and appointed a governor-general for Siberia. He placed strict controls on the Orthodox church. Since educated people were in great demand, Peter began the system of using foreign, especially Swedish and German, prisoners of war as officials. This led to the "Germanization" of the Russian bureaucracy, since these men enjoyed a generally better status than they had in their homeland and were abler than their Russian colleagues.

Peter divided all Russia into eight *gubernia* (provinces) of which Siberia and Perm were one. The governor of Siberia had his seat at Tobolsk and had the power of appointment of local officials. This relieved Moscow of detail work. The fiscal office was to check on the work of the governor and to report corruption. The officials of the fiscal office were afraid to report on anyone as highly placed as the governor of Siberia, so it was not until near the end of Peter's reign that the governor was reported. Peter had him hanged. Then instead of depending on a system to run Siberia, Peter began depending on men. Siberia was divided into regimental areas with each regiment being given the responsibility for a city and its surrounding area. The change was, of course, simply setting up one system within another. Peter toyed with the idea of having the Siberian middle class govern their cities and towns as chambers of burgomasters, but he abandoned the idea since nearly everyone in Siberia was poor. Instead, he sent honest wealthy men from Russia into Siberia to collect its taxes.

By 1700 good maps of Siberia had been prepared and Peter, with great vigor and interest, sent out further expeditions of which the greatest was the Messerschmidt mission. From 1719 to 1726 this mission wrote a thorough description of Siberia and its potential and also compiled an enormous report on the ethnology and languages of the vast region. Because of the decline in fur revenues, Peter decided to find out what alternative sources of wealth existed. Copper was discovered in the Urals, iron at Tobolsk, silver at Nerchinsk. The Demidov family became famous for its exploration and development of the metal wealth of the Urals. The development of mining in the Altai mountains was to make for a more aggressive policy toward China. In addition to rebellious Cossacks and army men, a stream of offenders was sent across the Urals as a means for providing a population for Siberia. (Siberia as a refuge for exiles started in the days of Boris Godunov, but until the time of Peter they had been mostly political exiles and prisoners of war. With Peter the exile settlers were added to by those guilty of criminal offenses.)

Peter's reforms were directed toward adjusting administrative abuse and slowness and toward the exploitation of minerals. Little, if anything, was done to develop agriculture and nothing was done for the natives. In effect, the reforms left the natives badly off, for with the dependence on the man in the field and not in Saint Petersburg, the government was less interested in protecting them. Natives were now subject to forcible conversion and were punished for holding to their own religious beliefs. Native slavery increased, and the peasants still formed the mass of the workers and army in Siberia.

On the Asiatic frontier Peter was interested primarily in trade and trade routes and not in the acquisition of territory. The grandiose plans and testaments of Peter I are mostly foreign fabrications. Soloviëv, the greatest of Russian historians, believes Peter's fundamental plan was to raise the Russian economy by developing a great trade with Europe. This is supported in the correspondence of Leibnitz with Peter, where we see the project for connecting the Baltic with the Caspian by waterway so as to tap the Baltic and the Indian trade. Since the official caravans returned 100 percent profit to Moscow, there is small wonder then that Peter made great efforts to develop the caravan trade with Peking as a government monopoly. It was under Peter that Ides, Ismailov, and Vladislavitch made their missions.

With the death of Peter in 1725, the bitter opposition to his radical reforms came into the open. Peter's separation of the judicial and executive functions in Siberia were reversed out of a desire to save money. Voevodas reappeared in the Siberian towns assuming their old functions while Peter's new city councils disappeared and European Uralia was detached from Siberia and placed under the gubernia of Kazan. Then in 1730 it was realized that these changes were not working and the Senate urged a return to the pre-Petrine system in entirety. The Senate report stated that the main difficulty was that local officials were unable to report to and be directly controlled by Saint Petersburg, and they urged that the Siberian Prikaz be reestablished under one man—a senator—who would then devote all his time to Siberian affairs.

The Prikaz was reestablished but under an already overloaded procurator general. In 1736 Siberia was divided into two independent parts (Tobolsk and Irkutsk), each part subordinate to the prikaz. This move proved unsuccessful. The administration of Irkutsk was indicted for bribery and corruption. This brought on a commission of investigation that revealed the mistreatment of natives and the corruption of officials. The Empress Anna (1730–1740), who believed that her position depended upon the support of the Russian nobility, tended to attribute the Siberian situation to the fact that many people of humble origin were in positions of power there. Her solution was to replace them with administrators of noble birth. The trouble, however, was that the overall system was so poor that even good men became demoralized in Siberian posts. When in 1741 Elizabeth became empress of Russia, her promise of an era of clemency did not apply to Siberia. Depravity and injustice ran riot. Extreme cruelty was shown to the natives for with the decline of furs they were neglected and brutalized. (Paulutskii of the Anadrysk outpost reported in 1746 that he was continually fighting the natives in his region and that his reprisals took the form of massacres.) Added to the mistreatment and the financial shambles was the persecution by the Orthodox church of "Old Believers" and un-Orthodox Christians settled in Siberia. It was not until Catherine II took the throne in 1762 that a firm central policy for the administration of Siberia was initiated. When Catherine became empress, there were three divisions of Siberia—Tobolsk, Eniseisk, and Irkutsk. Catherine added a fourth, Kolyma, and in 1781 combined all of the gubernias under the special administration of a lieutenant general for Siberia, in accord with the manifesto of 1775 that had criticized the old gubernias as too large and unwieldy for efficient administration. Financial matters were placed directly under a special treasury bureau. The Siberian Prikaz was abolished.

Paul I in his brief reign (1796–1801) combined Siberia into two gubernia—Tobolsk and Irkutsk—but otherwise tended to leave matters as they had been at Catherine's death. It was Alexander I who was to intitiate a thoroughgoing revision of the Siberian administration that had been so mishandled since the accession of Peter I.

Alexander I commenced his reign by sending new men into Siberia to make new plans in accord with local conditions, and then he appointed a governor-general to carry out these plans. Failing to do so but arguing that he lacked sufficient authority, the governor-general was then given complete control of military and civil affairs and ordered to encourage agriculture and to protect the peasant and the native. Selifontov, governor at Tobolsk, failed in his charge and Ivan Pestel replaced him in 1805. Pestel returned to Saint Petersburg in 1808 and for eleven years acted as governor-general of Siberia from that city. This was overlooked in the turmoil of the Napoleonic wars, but after the Congress of Vienna, the minister of the interior submitted a report on the deplorable conditions in Siberia. He pointed out that something had to be done and that the probable solution was local elective government with Saint Petersburg having the ultimate power.

Pestel was dismissed in 1819 and a remarkable man, Mikhail Speranski, was appointed as governor-general of Siberia. Speranski was of very humble origin. In 1790 he had gone to seminary in Saint Petersburg and afterward had distinguished himself as a teacher of mathematics and philosophy and as dean of the school. He had left his post to become secretary to a prominent aristocrat. When his protector lost his position, Speranski remained in the civil service and survived many changes due to his reputation for excellence. He became an aide to the Ministry of the Interior and in that capacity drafted government decrees and regulations in the beginning of the reign of Alexander I.

Alexander became fond of him and from 1807 to 1812 he was that tsar's most trusted adviser. But the atmosphere of monarchs is dangerous to breathe. Speranski's enemies played on his well-known fondness for French methods of administration and accused him of being pro-French so Alexander was forced to dismiss him. In 1819 he requested permission to return to the capital. This was not only granted but, in return for old times and old favors, Alexander made him governor-general of Siberia.

Speranski was not particularly interested in Siberia and he had no illusions about working wonders in the Siberian administration. He started methodically to investigate his new charge. He began at Tobolsk by inviting complaints to be made without fear of punishment or retribution. The conditions at Tobolsk were not so bad but he found Tomsk a sink of outrageous administration and corruption and Irkutsk the very apex of maladministration.

Loskutov, the senior policy official at Irkutsk, attempted to block Speranski's investigations. Speranski had him arrested on the spot and his iron rule of terror on the frontier was broken. Now the complaints from the peasants flooded in. The governors of Tomsk and Irkutsk were removed with imperial sanction, and in Irkutsk alone Speranski entered indictments against 216 officials. In March of 1820 the inspection tour was completed. In the year that remained of his appointment, Speranski tried to protect the interests of the natives and peasants, to establish justice, schools, and trade, and to encourage private enterprises and local self-government. The great difficulty was that while one could remove a poor official, he would often be replaced by a younger man trained in the same school of graft or by some man from Moscow who arrived in Siberia an honest man but who soon saw the personal advantages of corruption.

With his investigations completed and his reports in hand, Speranski returned to Saint Petersburg where a special Siberian Commission was established to consider his plans. The commission (one member was Count Alexis Arakcheev, a close consultant to the tsar,) approved the plans, and in 1822 legislation was enacted that was to bring the old Muscovite administration of Siberia into line with European Russia. Siberia was divided into an eastern and a western half. The western half had its main government at Tobolsk which supervised three gubernia—Tobolsk, Tomsk, and Omsk.

Each gubernia was further subdivided into units called *uezds* or *okrugi* (counties), and these in turn were subdivided into *volosti* (districts). Eastern Siberian headquarters was at Irkutsk with the three gubernia of Irkutsk, Eniseisk, and Yakutsk, plus three smaller administrative units. The eastern gubernia were also divided and subdivided into subordinate administrative units. The three former branches of administration—police, finance, and justice—continued, but to them were added *sovieti* or councils that operated at gubernia and uezd levels. These sovieti could not vote as Speranski had originally desired but could voice their opinions. Because of reaction in Saint Petersburg against too much local freedom, Speranski was able to get only the town mayors as elected officials. To see that the laws were carried out in a land habituated to lawlessness, supervisors (*striapchii*) were appointed with somewhat the function of inspectors-general. In effect the reforms of Speranski wiped out the old hand-to-mouth, arbitrary system of governing Siberia and replaced it with a carefully regulated net of officials working in accordance to law and ultimately responsible to the emperor through the governors-general. This reform was also designed to exploit the economic potentialities of Siberia by permitting, it was hoped, an atmosphere in which a sound agrarian economy could develop.

Finally, we must note the important new ordinances regarding the natives. Their rights were defined, special courts were established for them, their trade was safeguarded, and their taxes modified. They were given great cultural freedom within a general framework of Russification. Natives were divided into three groups. Town-dwelling and agricultural natives were classified as sedentary and given equal treatment with Russians. Migratory tribes were left alone under the administration of native courts. Reservations for their migrations were set aside and no interference was allowed except that they were responsible before Russian courts for capital crimes and any trade with them in alcohol was absolutely forbidden. The lowest level of natives was that of the fishers and wandering hunters who were free to go anywhere and to hunt anywhere and were exempt from taxes. The people on the border between Russia and China were treated as semi-independent units and allowed to trade as they pleased in return for granting protection to Russian envoys and trade caravans.

The final legislation of 1822, while not as enlightened as Speranski's original plans, were nevertheless a model of administration after what had gone on before. They acted as the foundation and the guide for the future development of the great Siberian region even though later administrators were to curtail much of what the commission of 1822 launched.

Central Asia under Peter and his Successors

At the turn of the eighteenth century the Russian empire claimed the land from the mouth of the Don River to the mouth of the Ural River. But its effective control ran only along the fortified line Poltava-Kharkov-Tambov-Sembirsk and along the lower Volga from Tsaritsyn (Kazan) to Astrakhan. The area outside the lines, while colonized, was by no means pacified and could not be pacified until Russia controlled both the tribes south of the Urals and the Central Asian khanates. The region, generally known as Turkestan from the Persian for "land of the Turkic peoples," consisted of the Kazak steppe and the khanates of Khiva and Kokand and the emirate of Bokhara. The region had no real government after the death of the last of the dynasty of Timur in the mid-sixteenth century. The people who lived there were the nomadic Kazaks who roamed from the Caspian Sea to the Tien Shan range and were called "Khirghiz" by the Russians to distinguish them from the Cossacks, although to compound the confusion there did exist a small Khirghiz group, and the Turkmen, Tadzhiks, and Uzbeks of the emirates and the khanates. All were mixtures of Iranian, Turk, and Mongol to a greater or less degree. The Kazaks were indifferent Moslems while the others were rigidly Moslem. As early as 1603 the Ural Cossacks under Nechai Starenskoi had raided into Khiva but had been bloodily repulsed.

It was under Peter that Russia, already committed in Siberia, began its penetrations of Central Asia. The great problem of the Central Asian frontier was the protection of the Russian trade and the Russian farmers from raids, for the Kazaks occupied good farming land and persistently raided the Caspian trade routes. It was a restless frontier where for 1,500 miles the Russian frontier ran with the Kazak lands. The Bashkirs were in an uproar most of the time, and the Kalmucks were uneasy allies of Russia. None of the tribes could be dealt with as a unit due to intratribal relationships. The ultimate solution seemed to be Russian political control of the Amu Darya region, the heartland of the Asian trade flowing to Russia. As early as 1700 the khan of Khiva had requested aid from Peter against his rival of Bokhara, but Peter, busy with Sweden, could send only moral support.

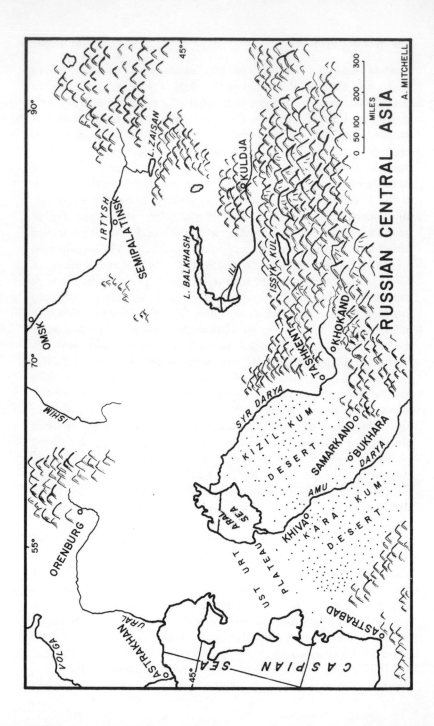

RUSSIAN CENTRAL ASIA

A. MITCHELL

MILES
0 50 100   200   300

90°

45°

L. ZAISAN

IRTYSH

SEMIPALATINSK

OMSK

70°

ISHIM

KULDJA

L. BALKHASH

ILI

ISSYK KUL

TASHKENT

KHOKAND

SYR DARYA

KIZIL KUM

DESERT

SAMARKAND

BUKHARA

DARYA

AMU

KHIVA

KARA KUM

DESERT

ARAL SEA

UST URT PLATEAU

ASTRABAD

55°

ORENBURG

URAL

ASTRAKHAN

VOLGA

CASPIAN SEA

45°

Then in 1713 a Turkman called Nefes came to Russian Astrakhan and struck up a friendship with Prince Samanov. Nefes suggested that Russia seize the valley of the Amu Darya. He stated that Khiva, from fear of the Russians, had changed that river's course so that it now drained into the Aral Sea instead of the Caspian but that the course of that river could again be altered to Russia's commercial benefit. Samanov took Nefes to Saint Petersburg to meet Alexander Beckovitch-Cherkassy, an adventurer, well established as a guards officer. Through Beckovitch, an audience was arranged with Peter I, who became greatly interested not only at the prospect of a water route into Central Asia but at the mention of gold in the valley of the Amu Darya. (At the same time the governor-general of Siberia was sending in reports of gold discoveries near Yarkand. It is possible that historians have confused Yarkand on the Turim River with the Yarkand of the Syr Darya, which no longer exists.) Peter authorized an expedition under Beckovitch that was to investigate the courses of the Amu Darya and a second expedition from Siberia to proceed via the Irtysh to find Yarkand. Beckovitch led a series of four expeditions between 1714 and 1717 along the eastern shore of the Caspian. His final expedition of 1717 reached Khiva, broke the resistance of the khan's forces, and entered the city. Then, fantastically enough, Beckovitch at the invitation of the khan of Khiva split his force into smaller units posted around the city. (It has been suggested that Beckovitch was mentally unbalanced during the last expedition by the news of the death of his wife and daughter.) Once his main force was broken into isolated detachments, the Khivans fell on them, slaughtered most of them, sent the remainder into slavery, gave Beckovitch's head to the khan of Bokhara as a warning present, and exhibited his stuffed body in the palace of the khan of Khiva.

The Siberian expedition to Yarkand had better success under Ivan Bukhgol. It had proceeded in 1715 along the Irtysh to Lake Yamish, a source of salt, where it built a fort. Now in the seventeenth century this region had been unsettled but in the eighteenth the Kalmucks began to push into the area. They were being pressed by Tse Wang Araptan, the nephew and successor to Galdan. The appearance of the Russians on the Irtysh aroused the Kalmucks and their leader, Chereng Danduch, requested that they withdraw. The Russians refused and their fort on the Yamish was blockaded and their supply routes cut. Hunger and disease caused the Russians to evacuate Yamish and retreat to the mouth of the river Om where they built the fort of Omsk in 1716.

Saint Petersburg now resorted to diplomacy. Having good relations with Araptan, they complained to him of the actions of Danduch and demanded the return of seized goods and of prisoners. This had results, for the second expedition of 1717 to Yamish was allowed to restore Fort Yamish. In 1718, a fort was established south of Omsk at Semipalatinsk, the site of an old Buddhist monastery. In 1720 the Russians advanced farther along the Irtysh to Lake Zaisan. Here the Kalmucks decided to call a halt to Russian expansion and, after a brief battle, the Russians agreed to retreat to Semipalatinsk and set that as the boundary line. However, by this time the Russians had created a line of posts along the Irtysh, Ural, Oren, and Ishim rivers and the outbreak of a tribal war in 1723 was to give them further opportunity to advance into Central Asia.

In 1723 the great khan of the Kazaks, Tauke, died and in the succession struggle a civil war broke out among the three hordes of the Kazaks (Great, Middle, and Small). The Jungarians took this as a grand opportunity to invade Turkestan and occupy Tashkent. Sultan Abdul Khair of the Small Horde asked Russia for aid and protection and his petition contained, unknown to his Kazaks, the request that his people be made Russian subjects. But Peter died in 1725 and Russia, wrangling over the succession, paid no attention to the petition. Meanwhile, the Kazaks found themselves able to defeat the Jungarians, whereupon the latter sent a petition for help to Saint Petersburg. The crown had been settled upon the Tsarina Anna and her government, now considering these petitions, was inclined to accept the petition of the Kazaks rather than that of the Jungarians, for it would mean greater security in the steppes and along the trade routes. Murza Tefkelov, diplomatist and linguist, was sent to meet Abdul Khair on the Irgiz River. Tefkelov found that Abdul was speaking largely for himself. In order to bring the other Kazak chiefs into agreement, Tefkelov, on Abdul's advice, distributed presents.

Now, the Kazak chiefs sat in council with Tefkelov and proposed that if Russia would restrain her Bashkir subjects from raiding Kazak territory, they, the Kazaks, would take care of the Jungarians. Tefkelov then told them this was a satisfactory proposition and that the Tsarina Anne would accept them as her subjects. The meeting broke into an uproar as many chiefs had desired only a military alliance, but a majority led by Abdul Khair finally took the oath of allegiance to the tsarina. This was the beginning of Russian dominion over the Kazaks. Tefkelov requested no tribute, instead guaranteeing subventions. A Kazak mission arrived in Saint Petersburg in 1734, bringing not only the Kazak oaths but the allegiance of the Kara Kalpaks, a small tribe at the mouth of the Syr Darya, and a request from Abdul Khair that Russia construct a fort in the Urals as a last-ditch refuge for the Kazaks—and more probably, Abdul Khair. The consideration of this last request led to a plan with a dual purpose of eventual domination of all the Kazaks and the protection of the Western Siberian-Southeast Russian frontiers. Ivan Kirilov proposed that both Bashkirs and Kazaks be pacified and brought under Russian control by using the one tribe against the other and sparing Russian soldiers in the process. Then a great fort and trade center was to be built in the Urals. It was to act not only as a barrier against nomad penetration but would anchor a line of forts that would both guard the frontier and keep the tribes separate from one another. In addition, the Jungarians were to be warned against attacking the Kazaks for fear of Russian reprisals. Finally, a flotilla would be built on the Aral Sea and the trade caravans from Asia would be organized over definite mapped and protected routes. The whole plan was initially upset by the violent resistance of the Bashkirs against the prospect of the Ural forts, and Kirilov, working from Ufa, had to devote his entire energy to the suppression of the revolt. He reported from Ufa on why the tribes were restless, pointing out the disturbing influence of non-Bashkirs, especially the Tatar Moslem clergy and the pressure on food and land caused by the high Bashkir birthrate. He proposed to take care of the latter problem by using the Bashkirs as a frontier police force. Kirilov died in 1737 but not until he had built his fort in the Urals, calling it Orenburg. His successor, Tatishchev, strengthened Orenburg and was immediately faced with the problem of a possible Kazak-Bashkir union. The Kazaks, in violation of their oath, raided Russian lands across the Urals.

The angry Bashkirs, impressed by this defiance of Russia, invited Abdul Khair into Bashkiria. In order to get past Orenburg and across the Urals, Abdul Khair proposed to Tatishchev that he cross and subdue the Bashkirs for Russia. Once the permission was granted, he crossed into Russian territory where he raided alike both loyal and disloyal Bashkirs. Retiring to his own region, he passed through Orenburg at a time when Tatishchev was absent. Acting on his earlier credentials from Tatishchev as a Russian ally, Abdul took unto himself the powers of the governor of Orenburg. Sitting as a court of justice, he confiscated Bashkir possessions to himself in the face of local Russian protests. Tatishchev was ordered back at once to Orenburg to repair his error and he returned in force to find that Abdul had left. Abdul returned on invitation to be given a great reception, apologies were tendered all around, Abdul took another oath, left his son as hostage for his conduct, and the danger of a Kazak-Bashkir union was averted.

At this particular time in the eighteenth century, Saint Petersburg was most interested in and involved with its policies in Poland and left the fate of Central Asia and Siberia in the hands of local administrators who had to police their frontiers by using the tribes. In 1739 Tatishchev was replaced at Orenburg by Urusov who continued the building of the forts amid Bashkir discontent. In 1740 a Bashkir uprising was quelled. One of the leaders fled to Abdul Khair, who refused to return him. So another Kazak congress was held at Orenburg, oaths were exchanged, and Abdul, in exchange for his friendship, requested a fort on the Syr Darya and the gift of cannon for use against his enemy of Khiva. Orenburg consented to this and prepared an expedition into the Syr Darya valley that was to bring Russia into an unexpected, although by no means its first, relationship with Persia.

Peter I, with his dream of control of the Asian trade through the Caspian Sea, had opened relations with Persia in 1716; this had turned out unsatisfactorily due largely to the Khivan disaster of Beckovitch. Then, when in 1721 Persians had looted Russian goods in the Caspian area, Peter decided to secure for Russia those Persian lands and towns along the southern Caspian. (This would protect Astrakhan, the depot for trade with China, Persia, and India.) After the Russo-Persian War of 1722–1724, Persia

ceded Astrabad, Chilan, Mazanderan, Shirvan, and Daghestan
(including Derbent, As-rabad, and Baku) to Russia. The entire
Caspian area was thus secured for Russia, incidentally beginning
the long Anglo-Russian rivalry in Persia. The return of these
areas to Persia was made by Anne in 1732 in return for commercial advantages in Persia and Central Asia. Anne wished to obtain Persian aid in the event of an impending war with Turkey,
a war that loomed precisely because of the Russian conquests in
the Caspian.

The Syr Darya expedition of 1741 set out at the time when
the great Nadir Shah was ruler of Persia. Nadir Shah was an empire builder who included among his conquests Tiflis, Delhi, and
Erzerum. When he turned to Central Asia, Bokhara surrendered
to him but Khiva decided to fight and asked its old enemy Abdul
Khair for aid. Khiva was defeated before Abdul Khair could
bring aid. With the prospect of Russian aid in view, Abdul left
Orenburg for Khiva and awaited the Russian Syr Darya expedition which, when it arrived, was requested by him to help negotiate with Persia toward a restoration of Khivan independence
with Abdul Khair as khan. These negotiations were entered into
and concluded satisfactorily and Orenburg could now turn its
attention again to Kazak-Kalmuck-Bashkir troubles.

In 1741 Neplivev, a smart young favorite, took charge of Orenburg and the frontier. He carried on the building of forts, attempted to attract peasant colonists into the area, and developed
Orenburg as a trade center. Fundamentally, however, he was
occupied with the problems of diplomacy vis-à-vis the tribes. In
1746 the Kazaks crossed the North Caspian on the ice and raided
Cossack settlements. This was Abdul Khair again ignoring his
allegiance, but Neplivev overlooked him in order to resume the
safe operation of caravans and to avoid any possible Kazak-
Jungar union. This was Abdul's last action for he soon died.
Orenburg backed his eldest son, Nur Ali, for the khanate, got him
elected, and sent a deputation to Saint Petersburg for confirma-
tion. (Meanwhile, the Jungarian leader offered all Turkestan to
Nur Ali in return for his sister. Nur Ali wavered and was only
saved from his dilemma when the girl died in 1750.)

In the middle of the eighteenth century the tribal problem

again rose to a head as the khan of Khiva began raids on the Russian frontier. Tevkelev (Neplivev's chief of staff) began reprisals using native troops and Russian auxiliaries. The trouble was that the reprisals made no distinction of guilt among the tribes and the peaceful Kazaks suffered as well. This turned the friendly Kazaks into brigands, and the whole frontier erupted in 1755 with both Kazaks and Bashkirs fighting. More than 1,000 Russians were killed.

Orenburg blamed the uprising on the Moslem mullahs, but the more probable cause was Russian encroachments on the lands of both tribes. Neplivev now mustered as large a force as he could, held it in reserve, and then by forged letters aroused tribes subject to the Bashkirs to revolt. The Bashkirs asked Orenburg's permission to send a punitive expedition across the Ural River. Neplivev consented and secretly withdrew all the frontier guards leaving the Bashkirs to face not only their own unruly allies but also the Kazaks. In the resulting Bashkir-Kazak war, Neplivev waited until both sides were bled white in the slaughter, then stepped back in and closed the frontier to find that only the Bashkir half of his problem was solved and that additional trouble was brewing among the Kazaks.

In order to understand the continuing eruption of the Kazak tribes, it is necessary to turn our attention back to the year 1745 and to the Jungarian state of Kuldja. In 1746 Galdan Chereng of Jungaria died and one of the claimants to his power requested aid from Peking. China refused. The claimant successfully raided into Chinese territory, and China now determined on a reprisal that would, once and for all, break Jungarian power. In 1756 China struck with great force and it is estimated that perhaps one million Jungarians were killed. Jungaria never recovered and it became Chinese territory. Chinese forces in pursuit crossed the Ili passes into Turkestan and the mountains south of the Ili to Tashkent. Orenburg tried to get the Kazaks to stem this Chinese advance, but an ineffectual governor by his curt treatment of Nur Ali merely encouraged that ruler to play both sides covertly while overtly raiding Russian territory. Then, in the midst of this, trouble arose with the hitherto peaceful Kalmucks and again we have to turn our attention backward.

In 1724 Khan Ayuka of the Volga Kalmucks died. The Russians, who had always been wary of a possible union between the Volga Kalmucks and the Crimean Tatars, decided to back their own candidate. They had their man baptized as a Christian with some vague hope that this would help influence a Buddhist tribe. The Russian candidate was elected and immediately returned to lama Buddhism. Nevertheless, he was repudiated by a great number of his people who elected another leader. Civil war resulted and in 1735 the Russian puppet fled. His rival made peace with Russia and proved a loyal vassal, even supporting Russia in the Turkish war of 1735–1739. Nevertheless, Russia, as a matter of standard practice, retained its own candidate at Saint Petersburg. (This pan-Orthodoxy was injurious to Russia's tribal policies. It presented the paradox of a strong government with control over the Orthodox church allowing that church very great powers against the government's own best interests in Central Asia.) Then in 1741 Chereng Danduch of the Kalmucks died. The Russian command at Astrakhan (from where Kalmuck policy was administered) maneuvered his widow out of the throne that she had seized and placed Danduch Trishi in as khan in 1751.

Danduch Trishi died in 1761 and was succeeded by his son Ubasha. Ubasha was angry at the Russians for their failure to show a proper gratitude to his people for their aid against Turkey. Furthermore, he and his people were tired of being used as shock troops on the frontier in behalf of Russia, and he began to listen attentively to the advice of the lamas to break away from Russia and return to Asia. In 1771 the great Kalmuck migration began. Passing through Kazak territory (the Kazaks refused Orenburg's request to stop the movement), a quarter million Kalmucks reached China after an eight month trip.

Hardly had this occurred when the entire frontier blew up in Pugachev's Rebellion. The appearance of the imposter Pugachev with his claims to the Russian throne brought rebellion to the entire Urals-Volga region and drew into it all non-Russian peoples but the Kazaks. When Catherine II had put down the rebellion, she seriously turned her attention to the tribal problems of Central Asia. Catherine was to bring direction of these affairs back to Saint Petersburg from local hands. Catherine's infatuation with

Rousseau's concepts of the simplicity and grandeur of the savage nature influenced her native policy. Asia appealed to her imagination as a place in which to carry out a liberal colonial policy.

Early in her reign she had ordered a census of Siberian natives and had issued a manifesto that all Russian subject peoples were to be treated kindly and violators were to be punished if the natives complained. She attempted to protect native interests from Russian encroachment by establishing reservations. She invited tribal chiefs to Saint Petersburg. She referred to the area as the Siberian Kingdom and placed a throne in Tobolsk. She now viewed Central Asia in the same light. She forbade punitive expeditions (this was later retracted) and ordered her officials at Orenburg and Astrakhan to clean up their administrations and place the nomads on the road to civilization. The Kazaks were to be taught how to use bread and to make hay and were to be made into a sedentary people. Kazak schools were to be built and to be staffed by Moslem scholars while Russian money was to build Moslem mosques. These measures were ordered in 1782 as a move to counteract Turkish propaganda that the empress of Russia was an enemy to Islam. Catherine would now claim a policy of religious tolerance and of friendship with Moslems.

To further help the natives, she established a series of "frontier courts" made up of frontier people to adjudicate disputes between Russians and Cossacks. In 1785 she appointed a new administration at Orenburg under Igelstrom. His instructions were to initiate a new Kazak governing policy. Nur Ali was now dead and Orenburg urged the Kazaks not to elect a khan but to establish a general tribal government. The tribes, less their aristocracy, gathered to consider this and took an oath of loyalty, which they kept for two years. The Kazak aristocracy was upset by the change, however, and the daughter of Nur Ali seduced Igelstrom and got him to rescind the move and appoint a khan. Most of the tribes resented this about-face, and a certain unrest again became evident and remained so. Despite the Russian hold on the tribal peoples, Central Asia remained insecure and peripheral. Still following their ancient rhythm of life, the nomads and seminomads of the hordes and tribes basically acknowledged only the most shadowy allegiance to one or another of their great neighbors—Russia and China, while the settled populations of the once great cities—Merv, Khiva, Bokhara, Samarkand—owed their duty to their own feudal rulers. Not until the middle of the nineteenth century was Russia able to secure her settlers along the frontier of southern Siberia and begin the occupation of the rich lands of the steppes.

THE PACIFIC AND NORTH AMERICA

Kamchatka

Now barred from southern expansion by the treaty with China, Russia again turned east and her frontiersmen penetrated the last bit of continental Asia left them, the peninsula of Kamchatka. The conquest of Kamchatka was slow because it was barred by the Anadyr region, which was so barren that the Russians preferred to leave it alone. In 1649–1650 they had constructed a fort on the Anadyr, but the Chuckchee and Yukaghirs of the region put up a tremendous resistance. (The Chuckchee were only quelled in the mid-nineteenth century.) The way to the Anadyr was hard and the route was only garrisoned by a few men. But news came, via the Koriaks of the Penzhina region, of a great peninsula farther south and east and the Cossack Vladimir Atlasov was sent by the voevoda at Yakutsk to obtain information.

Atlasov, poorly educated but tough and observant, set out in 1696 to coast the Bering Sea. One of his detachments went into Kamchatka for a short distance. In 1697 Atlasov and Lucas Morosco, another Cossack frontiersman, set out along the Bay of Shelekov toward Penzhina, where Atlaslov seized three Koriak settlements which he used as a base. Heading south he ran into a new kind of native—fishermen and hunters and very hard fighters who would accept only iron in barter. Pressing south into the unknown against continuous native resistance, Atlasov compounded his troubles by his brutal treatment of the people he met. His Yukaghirs deserted him, and he was forced to build boats and take to the Kamchatka River. When he turned back to the west coast, he had to fight his way back through Koriak territory. He left a small garrison behind in Kamchatka while he returned to Anadrysk. This garrison was forgotten for three years and when it tried to return it was massacred on the way back.

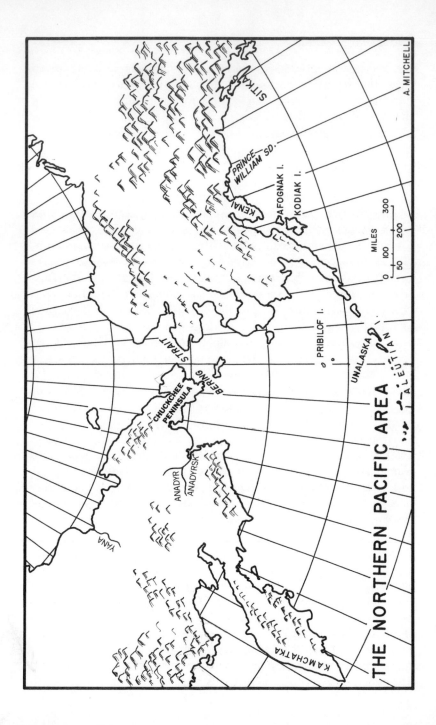

THE NORTHERN PACIFIC AREA

A. MITCHELL

SITKA

PRINCE-
WILLIAM SD.

KENAI

AFOGNAK I.

KODIAK I.

MILES

0 50 100 200 300

PRIBILOF I.

UNALASKA

ALEUTIAN

CHUCKCHEE
PENINSULA

BERING
STRAIT

ANADYR

ANADYRSK

YANA

KAMCHATKA

The Russians in Kamchatka, however, had stood on the western water marches of the Pacific and faced North America.

The Pacific Empire

Toward the end of his reign, Peter I had been urged by his scientific advisers to discover a northwest passage to India and to uncover the relationship of Asia to America. Vitus Bering, a Dane in Russian service, was instructed to build a shipping base in Kamchatka and from there to undertake voyages to the north and east. In July 1728, after a year of preparation, Bering sailed from Kamchatka in two small vessels going north as far as he dared which was to sixty-four degrees of latitude and then turning back without having come upon the American coast. He had actually passed between the two continents without realizing that he was traversing a strait. The discovery of the North American coast came with the Russian expedition of 1730. While mapping the coastline of the Chuckchee Peninsula, the expedition was blown east by strong winds and for two days lay in sight of the Alaskan coast without being able to land on it. Their reports confirmed Bering's hopes and a series of voyages was planned, under the direction of the Russian Academy of Sciences. These were intended first to see if it were possible to trace the coast of the "Icy Sea" and find a water route from Archangel to Kamchatka and second, to confirm the relation to Asia of the American coast.

Between 1734 and 1738 a number of remarkable voyages by small boats were undertaken along the Arctic rim of Russia. Despite scurvy, cold, and hostile natives, they succeeded in mapping the way along the Arctic coast. Bit by bit through the eighteenth century the Russians were gaining accurate information on the coasts and islands of the North Pacific. In 1741 the most important information came through the second voyage of Vitus Bering in which one of the ships of that disastrous voyage reached Sitka Sound on the North American mainland. Now provided with navigational information, the freebooters and pioneers of Eastern Siberia began the exploration and exploitation of the Aleutian Islands. As the wealth of the Aleutian furs began to dwindle from the unrestricted hunting during the 1770s, it became obvious that the great continent farther east would have to be opened up if the trade were to survive.

The Russian-American Company

The idea of a Russian-American Company to parallel the work, objectives, and, it was hoped, the profits of the East India Company was born in the mind of the fur merchant Gregory Shelekhov. Beginning in 1777 he was increasingly active in pioneer voyages to the Kurile and Aleutian islands and as the years passed he noticed that the fur yield from this area was diminishing.

Determined to find out at first hand why this should be, he left Okhotsk in 1783 and wintered in the Aleutian Islands. He then went on to Unalaska and finally to Kodiak Island, which he made his headquarters. The single native found on Kodiak was feasted and given presents and he became of great value as a guide and scout for Shelekhov's party. Shelekhov, in an attempt to make friends with the Koniags of the vicinity of Kodiak, sent those of his own men who spoke a related language to offer peace and trade.

The Koniags, however, had had bad experience with fur traders. They refused and even attempted to destroy Shelekhov's small post. Shelekhov struck back by bombardment from his small vessels. The natives panicked. Some were taken as hostages and a small fort was built on Kodiak. Shelekhov was a far-sighted man, however, and once he had beaten off the initial attack on his post, he made every effort to deal with the Kodiak Islanders on a fair and patient basis. He gradually convinced them that his only interest was in the fur trade. With some mutual confidence restored, Shelekhov sent a small expedition to Kenai Inlet where the natives proved to be friendly. One of his own native agents deserted him though and fled to Kenai, raising a revolt which put the Russian post there in danger and caused the traders to build still a third post on Afognak Island. In 1787, after three years of this kind of frustrating business, Shelekhov returned to Siberia with a haul of furs. He proposed to the governor-general at Irkutsk that the tsar's government permit him and his partner Golikov to organize a company to monopolize the trade in the Aleutian-Alaskan region. This company was to be subordinate only to the governor-general himself at Irkutsk and was to have the privilege of direct communications with Saint Petersburg. (Shelekhov had had too much experience with the Siberian administration to want to be at the mercy of its agents.)

The proposal envisaged far more than a mere trading company. Permission was requested to hire military specialists, gunners, navigators, and sailmakers. Around this professional core a native army and fleet were to be organized. A number of political and criminal exiles were to be used as a labor force to build a port better than the difficult harbor of Okhotsk. This port was to be a trading center where the goods of China, America, Japan, and the Philippines were to be exchanged. The port was to be fed from its own grain supply grown by farmer-settlers supplied to the new company by the government of Russia. The governor-general, highly impressed by this plan, sent the report and request on to Saint Petersburg. He knew of the voyages of Cook and Vancouver and of Spanish visits to Nootka Sound, and he did not wish the English or Spanish to seize this territory. The high commercial officials of Catherine the Great were equally impressed and the plan was passed on to the empress. Catherine immediately turned it down. Her ostensible reason was that as an advocate of free trade she would never grant this kind of monopoly. Privately she admitted that she thought Shelekhov was bluffing as to the prospects of such a company and she also was disturbed at the reports that had been reaching her of the brutality practiced toward the North Pacific tribes by the pioneers. These reasons all played some part in her refusal, but the fundamental reason was the difficult international situation. This was the period of Russia's war with Turkey and of strife in Poland.

Catherine wished to avoid anything that would antagonize Great Britain, whose neutrality was needed in both Poland and Turkey. Catherine had a pretty good idea that a Russian commercial company operating on the western boundaries of Canada would vex the British. She was deeply interested in Pacific North America, and in 1787 she ordered four ships of the Baltic fleet to proceed to the North Pacific to investigate Alaska and the Kuriles. The Swedish war killed this plan, but Captain Joseph Billings, who had served with Cook, did proceed to chart the Aleutians in 1790 for Russia. This was the same year that Shelekhov, who had been, in the interim, sending supplies to his fort on Kodiak, requested permission to explore the American coast in an effort to discover a passage from the Kolyma River to the Alaskan coast. This was denied and Shelekhov took it upon himself to organize a smaller expedition. In 1791 he sent Delarov, the manager of his company on Kodiak, to explore Chugat Bay (Prince William Sound). This area proved rich in beavers, and Shelekhov now began sending other small groups into the North American coast. Catching wind of this, other traders began to trap and buy on the North American mainland. They were followed by Spanish, French, British, and American shipmasters. The Russians, however, who had pioneered the territory, made a practice on all their landings on the coast of leaving behind them copper plates engraved with messages claiming the territory for Russia. Unable through more than a decade to obtain an imperial charter granting him monopolistic rights of trade, Shelekhov kept organizing companies of his own to swallow up the competition in the hope that he could arrive at a virtual monopoly of the trade without royal sanction.

In order to operate effectively he had to have a permanent manager in Alaska while he stayed in Russia, someone who could be trusted to run the whole show thousands of miles away. He picked a merchant who had been trading with the Chuckchee and who was temporarily bankrupt because of business losses. In 1791 this new manager, Alexander Baranov, arrived in Kodiak to replace Delarov. Baranov, who was to be the genius of Russia in Northwest America, was a fount of energy. Hardly had he arrived when he started his men exploring not only around the Alaskan peninsula but across it. He established friendly relations with visiting Spanish ships in Chugat Bay. Since tribal warfare meant an end to the fur supply, he mediated wars between the tribes of the Kenai region. Between 1793 and 1795 he built three ships with the materials at hand in order to increase his trading range.

Baranov's major problem was the relationship with the powerful trading concerns that Shelekhov had not managed to absorb. The most prominent of these was the firm of Lebedev-Lastochkin, discoverers of the Pribilov seal beds, who in 1791 established their own post in Kenai Inlet. In 1793 this firm asked Baranov to stay out of the area. Naturally he refused, and a small trade war began in which each of the companies used native allies to raid the others' boats and stores. The result was almost complete ruination of all Russian business activities in Alaska. The news of this ruinous competition helped Saint Petersburg to decide that Alaska, if it were to prove profitable, would have to be exploited by a single company. Meanwhile Shelekhov was maintaining his activities toward influencing the government. In 1793 he asked that Orthodox missionaries be sent to Alaska in order to give his enterprise an air of permanence and respectability. Baranov built a church but balked at Shelekhov's plan to build a grandiose capital on the mainland of Alaska to be called Slavo Rossia. The question of building anything of this proportion in what was savage wilderness where crops could not be grown struck Baranov as singular.

In 1795 Gregory Shelekhov died and the fate of his company and of his plans hung in the balance until his son-in-law Count Rezanov, who had taken over charge of the operations, proved to be equally as energetic as Shelekhov. In addition Russia was under a new ruler, Paul I, who, receiving favorable reports from Irkutsk about the operations of the Baranov-Shelekhov company and sensing the importance of Alaska, resolved to give the company a favorable position in the trade. Unlike his mother, Catherine II, Paul was bitterly anti-English. He blamed the British for the failure of the First Coalition against Bonaparte and for the loss of strategic Malta. He welcomed a strong Alaskan position for Russia as a means of striking at England, at least commercially, where it was assumed the nation of shopkeepers would be hurt the most.

Therefore Paul announced that he welcomed the creation of a single Alaskan company. This gave Shelekhov's competitors time to avoid liquidation by joining him, and in 1797 the United American Company was organized. It was dominated by the Shelekhov organization. Paul's advisers then recommended that this coalition become a single monopolistic company because such an outfit would acquire a large Pacific fleet that would be handy to Russia in case of war. This recommendation spelled the death knell of any individual companies left, for in 1799 the Russian American Company was chartered under the protection of the emperor of Russia. All other companies were to come under this

charter or go out of business, and one-third of the shares were
to go to Shelekhov's heirs. The charter of the company was broad
and useful. The company was given the use of all Russian estab-
lishments on the Northwest Coast of America from fifty-five degrees north to the Bering Straits. It alone could exploit the
Aleutian and Kurile Islands and all other islands on the Northeast Pacific. It could tap any resource in addition to furs. It could
settle and fortify any place within the area of the charter. It
could trade with neighboring countries, if they approved and if
the emperor consented. (This was a reference to China and to
Japan.) Baranov was to be chief administrative officer of the
American colonies, and Rezanov was to be the chief liason officer
between the Russian government and the company. The headquarters were transferred from Yakutsk to Saint Petersburg and
many powerful people including members of the Imperial family
took shares in the company. The financial participation of the
Imperial family and the very broad nature of the government
charter have led to a contradictory set of opinions about the
company. Soviet historians tend to view it as a tool of Saint
Petersburg in Russian expansion while non-Soviet historians
tend to view it as a reasonably private enterprise regarded be-
nevolently by the Russian government. The fact seems to be that
it was, primarily and fundamentally, a private commercial company whose relationship to Saint Petersburg was something akin
to the old relationship between Moscow and the Stroganovs. The
company was to take all the risks and all the blame and share the
profits. In return the government guaranteed to keep all Russian
competition away and to give aid and assistance, within reasonable limits, meaning within limits that cost the government practically nothing. In the five years between the death of Shelekhov
and the creation of the Russian-American Company, Baranov had
been active in trading, building forts, and buying or beating out
smaller competitors. When the new company was announced, he
decided to found his headquarters at Sitka Bay. This was done
in 1799, but, beginning in 1800, the Sitka settlement was visited
by British and American ships that, to Baranov's disgust, were
able to trade more successfully than he with the natives. The
American ships traded whiskey and guns, the British ships
traded better goods than either the Russians or Americans, and

both Americans and British asked lower prices. Baranov's position on Sitka was precarious, mostly due to food shortages and to the enmity of the Kolosh Indians, so he returned to Kodiak. Kodiak was also in a precarious food situation. In 1800 the Kolosh sacked Sitka. It took until 1804 for the company to raise an expedition to retake that settlement, which was renamed New Archangel. With the founding or refounding as it were of New Archangel, the company had 470 men scattered through thirteen posts in Russian America, and it was having increasing difficulty maintaining the men and the posts because of a chronic shortage of food. It was also having trouble with the natives because of the interference of the Russian clergy with traditional native practices. There was, in addition, a certain resentment of the clergy among the Russian settlers because of well-meant but misguided attempts to reform their rather noisome habits. This human problem could be controlled, but the food supply of the North American colonies was a desperate thing.

The dangerous and expensive route from the port of Okhotsk to Alaska was itself at the end of a long and expensive route from Western Siberia. Nerchinsk barred Russia from the Amur Valley where food could be grown. It would have to prove possible to do one of three things if the Alaskan posts were to continue. The company would have to find a source of food close at hand; it would have to find winter ports and food in Japan; or it would have to devise a profitable means of shipping directly from Saint Petersburg to Alaska. Rezanov decided to make all three attempts to see which would work out. With the blessing of Alexander I, and with two ships under Captains Krusenstern and Lisiansky, Rezanov started from Kronstadt as chief of a mission to Japan. The previous attempt to open relations with Japan had been in 1792. Then Delarov, Shelekhov's old executive officer, had sent a party of shipwrecked Japanese from the Aleutians to Yakutsk with the suggestion that they be returned to Japan as a lever for opening negotiations for a winter port. The Russian government was not interested and sent the inexperienced Captain Laxman on a voyage to Japan that was not successful except for an official pass Laxman received to enter Nagasaki.

Rezanov left Kronstadt, bound for Hawaii. At Hawaii his two ships parted, one going to Kodiak and the other with Krusenstern to Kamchatka and then to Nagasaki. Rezanov got nowhere with his negotiations at Nagasaki and decided that Japan would have to be opened by force, if possible. Rezanov then took a company ship in Kamchatka for the North Pacific crossing. The tour of inspection went from Kamchatka to the Pribiloffs (where sealing had stopped due to the extermination of the herds), to Unalaska, to Kodiak, and to Sitka. At Sitka the winter of 1805–1806 was spent effecting reforms. The clergy were ordered to study native languages, a mixed court was set up to deal with native disputes, a school was established, and some children were ordered back to Russia for trade schooling. The winter of 1805–1806 was a hard one, and Rezanov became desperate about replenishing his food supply. In February 1806, he sailed south along the coast to San Francisco. Despite Spanish efforts to prevent him from doing so, he entered the harbor. To Commandant Arguello he announced himself as the governor of Russian-America who, enroute to negotiate directly with the Spanish headquarters at Monterey, had to stop in San Francisco to get provisions. By a judicious distribution of gifts, through a genuine friendship with Doña Concepcion Arguello, daughter of the commandant of San Francisco, and because of the friendship of the missionaries in California, Rezanov received his supplies. Don Jose Arillaga, governor of California, who had come up from Monterey to meet Rezanov, informed him that the Spanish were quite willing to sell supplies to Russian America, but this would have to be done unofficially since Spain was an ally, although unwilling, of France and France was at war with Russia. The result was that Rezanov arrived back at Sitka in June 1806 with a shipload of foodstuffs from California.

Once back in Sitka, he could now set in operation still another part of his vast scheme to open food sources and winter ports. He sent two captains, Kvostov and Davidov, in two company ships, on a mission to raid parts of northern Japan. His theory was that if the island of Saghalien were occupied and the ports of Hokkaido raided, the threatened loss of their fishing areas in the Okhotsk and Northern Pacific would force the Japanese to trade with the "new" Russian base on Saghalien. He had informed Saint Petersburg that he intended to use force on Japan, but that capital, involved in the Napoleonic wars, sent no reply to what seemed to it to be a fantastic scheme. Rezanov persisted. He issued orders from Okhotsk in late 1806 to his small ships to raid through the Kuriles and in Saghalien, to seize Japanese shipping, destroy stores, to treat the natives decently, and to capture Japanese males, priests, and idols, all of which were to be resettled on the northwest coast of the New World. Then, since he was proceeding without any sanction from his home government and he did not want the responsibility of starting a war with a foreign power yet he wanted to see the plan carried through, he issued completely contrary orders to Kvostov and Davidov and left Okhotsk without clearing up the contradictions. So his captains proceeded on the basis of their original orders. In 1806–1807 the two small ships raided and destroyed Japanese settlements in the Kuriles and in Saghalien. The amount of actual physical damage done was inconsiderable. The effect on Japanese policy was considerable. The effort to open the Japanese trade failed. Rezanov, who now knew the company could not sustain itself in Northeast Siberia and Alaska unless it had secure trading and supply bases, went to Saint Petersburg to plead his case, but he died enroute, in Krasnoiarsk in 1807.

During these years of 1805–1807 Baranov had been struggling along, short of food, ships, and crews. In 1807 he decided that if the company were to survive at all in the North Pacific and America now that the Japanese attempt had failed, it would have to open routes directly across the Pacific to China and directly down the California coast.

In 1807 Captain Hagemeister, who was to succeed Baranov as head of the company, took a company ship to the Sandwich Islands. There he was greeted warmly by King Kamehameha I, and he was able to secure food. From 1807–1815 the company, using American skippers under charter as navigators and captains, opened the famous Alaska-Hawaii-Canton trade. Furs from Alaska went to China via Hawaii, which was used as a depot for food and water and a source of rare trade woods. In 1815 Baranov made an effort to occupy one of the Hawaiian islands as a permanent naval station for the company (and Russia), but the intervention of the British and Americans in the islands resulted in his agents being expelled. With Japan and Hawaii closed to the company and with what trade there was in

Alaska becoming the object of an intense rivalry between American, British, and Russian traders, the only hope for the company to be able to supply its posts in Alaska and the Aleutians with food lay in Spanish California.

By 1808 Baranov's men had made a preliminary survey of the coast of California and had selected Bodega Bay as a likely spot for a post. Here Fort Ross (Rossia) was established, strategically located where it was hoped to raise grain and cattle and set up a boat repair shop. The Spanish in California protested; but when they found out the Russians desired the post at Fort Ross only to raise food, they permitted it to remain there (although the northern limits to Spanish California had never been defined). Russian ships were permitted to trade as far south as San Pedro. When Governor-General Arillaga, the friend of the Russians, died, the situation changed. Upon orders of the viceroy in Mexico City, the new Governor-General Pablo Vicente De Sola of California ordered that Fort Ross be destroyed. The company temporized and negotiated with the authorities in California, but it became obvious that Fort Ross was a failure as a food base. In addition, the entire line of Russian posts in North America was under pressure from English colonization of the Oregon country and from the Americans pouring into northern California goldfields. Fort Ross was sold in 1841. Fearful lest a discovery of gold in Alaska would inundate the few Russian posts in Russian America with Canadian gold seekers, the decision was taken to sell the Alaskan territories. It was obvious that Russian commercial interests were suffering heavy losses in America. Furthermore, the growth and consolidation of British America placed on the threshold of the outnumbered Russians an energetic and well-supplied population that looked with longing on the Alaskan territory and could not have been stopped from seizing it if they chose to use force to do so. Finally, it was obvious to Saint Petersburg by the first quarter of the nineteenth century that Russia's true and main interests lay in the mainland of Asia and that the great question was not how to supply Alaska but how to maintain and supply Eastern Siberia. This meant that again the question of the use and possession of the Amur valley was paramount. In order to concentrate on this question of Siberia and the Amur, it was desirable to retreat from the American continent but in so doing to place between English and Russian possessions the buffer of a friendly power. Hence the decision to sell Alaska, at a ridiculously low price, to the United States. The American-Northern Pacific venture was over in 1867 and Russia could then devote her attention wholly to the administration, colonization, and protection of her lands and frontiers in Siberia and Central Asia.

On Nomenclature

Between the Volga River and the frontiers of China proper and from the Arctic Ocean to the khanates of Central Asia, the Russians came into contact with a great variety of peoples. These ranged from small, quite primitive groups like the Finnish-speaking natives of the lower Ob through more advanced tribes like the Koriaks of the Kamchatka Peninsula to large and sophisticated groups like the semi-Sinicised Mongol confederations and the literate, civilized Islamic populations of the emirates and khanates. As far as possible I have used those names which the Russians used in referring to these various peoples. But the Russians often used the wrong name. People call themselves one thing while outsiders—whether Russian or Chinese or other—call them another. Many Russian names were only approximations. *Kalmuck* (*Kalmyck*) is an example. The variant names for Eastern and western Mongols as used by those who came into contact with them can be seen on p. 82. Another example is that of the *Polovtsi,* who were *Comans* or *Cumans* to the Eastern Latins and *Kipchak* to Arabic-speaking peoples. Still another example is *Turk. Turkish* refers to a language family, a branch of Altaic, and a rather large variety of peoples of various names are Turkish by virtue of the fact that they speak one or another of the *Turkic* languages. The *Turks* were the *T'u-chueh* to the Chinese. The *Uighurs* who speak a Turkish language were the *Hui-hu* of the Chinese. The very language name itself gave rise to the vast geographical denomination *Turkestan.*

Often native names were badly transliterated. The same tribe would be known to the Chinese by one name, while the Russians used another. Sometimes the Russians used two names for the same group, often confusing the name of a tribe with the name for their territory. That patrimony of Khan Batu known as the *Khanate of the Golden Horde* was also the *Kipchak Khanate*. But the *Kipchak Khanate* was itself a composite of patrimonies of which Batu's *Western Kipchak* or *Golden Horde* was but a part, while his brother Orda held the *Eastern Kipchak* or *White Horde* realm. Another brother, Sheban, ruled the *Shebanids* or *Uzbegs*. Nogai, a grandson of Juchi, had his own following as we have seen, and another descendent of Juchi, Ureng, was leader of the *Crimean Tatars*. All paid allegiance to the khan of the Golden Horde at Sarai. *Tatar* is another case in point. Properly speaking *Tatar* is a Turkish language. The Russians confused this to the point of calling many non-Tatar steppe people Tatars, and this, plus a similar very old linguistic confusion from the Chinese, led to the West using the name *Tatar* for practically all of the nomadic peoples between the Chinese and Russian borders including Mongols and even extending the name to cover all of continental East Asia.

The entire question of identification and nomenclature is an extremely interesting one and has been surveyed in the works of Sinor (92, 93) and in L. Krader, *Peoples of Central Asia* (Bloomington, University of Indiana Press, second edition, 1966), whose prose is often impenetrable but whose information is sound and useful, and in M. Levin and L. Potapov's, *The Peoples of Siberia* (Chicago, University of Chicago Press, 1964), which, while concerned mainly with recent and modern times, is most valuable.

Bibliography

BIBLIOGRAPHICAL NOTE

The history of the Russian empire in Siberia, Central Asia, the North Pacific, and North America rests upon archives in Russia, China, Japan, Great Britain, Spain, the United States, and Rome. When the history of Russia to the time of the conquest of the khanate of Sibir is added, as it must be in order to gain a comprehensive picture, the variety and scope of the known sources and secondary works are simply enormous. In addition, the number of languages in which they are written comprises, possibly, the greatest number of languages needed to explore any history. They include Russian, Old Slavonic, Bulgarian, Greek, Chinese, Japanese, Mongol, Latin, French, German, English, Spanish, Persian, Armenian, Syrian, and Arabic. No one person or group of persons has as yet explored all the sources or even all the secondary works. On the other hand, there have been published many bibliographies, indices, collections of documents, chronicles, voyages and travels, collections of correspondence, monographs, articles, and general works that ably treat some period or subject of this vast history. These publications are sufficient and varied enough for both the purposes of the serious scholar and the interested reader who wish, each in his own way, to read further. The principle of this note is highly eclectic—to cite sufficient selected important works so as to—in the order cited: (1) enable the general reader to explore his interests more fully in works printed in English, French, or German; (2) lead the interested scholar into a fuller range of printed materials in a number of languages.

Availability has not been a consideration. A goodly number of works cited can be found only in a limited number of major libraries, while other works cited can be found in any good university or major public library. Much Soviet scholarship has been printed in limited quantities and is difficult to find. Overall there is considerable Soviet scholarship on this subject. There is much less from the Chinese side and there is very little work based on both Russian and Chinese sources that deals with the periods prior to the nine-teenth century. Archival work in the Soviet Union is not always fruitful, if only for the reason that many archives have been destroyed over the years. In certain instances, archives, especially provincial ones, are not open for use. But printed works are available (and in some instances may be borrowed) from the great Lenin Library. The Helsinki Library, which was in Tsarist times a repository, contains large numbers of prerevolutionary printed works. Archival work in mainland China is out of the question. There are available some very full printed collections of documents in Chinese, but to be productive they have to be laboriously read in their entirety because the methods of arrangement were not, normally, by area or subject. The arrange-ment of this note corresponds to the major divisions of the text. Many of the general works cited cover a great deal more than a single subject; however, they are cited only once under the first appropriate heading. Wherever there is a translation of value from Russian or an Oriental language, the translation is noted.

Anyone approaching the subject for the first time should read Barthold (1). Vasily Barthold was a great Orientalist: a first authority on Central Asia and its people and history. His work is concerned with the geographical and intellectual discovery of Asia by Russia and Europe and with the literature of that discovery. Each chapter deals with an important phase in the history of the discovery and includes a full bibliography mainly of periodical literature. The trans-lator has included additional bibliography as an appendix. Both the bibliographies—the author's and the translator's—are now partially out-of-date and many items are difficult to find, but the basic text remains a splendid overview.

THE LAND

Kerner's work (2) is a very detailed history of the geography of Russian expansion to the Pacific Ocean and to the Black and Caspian seas. It is solidly based on Russian sources, has excellent sketch maps, and details all of the routes of discovery across Eurasia. There are two books in English on the historical and physical geography of Russia that should be consulted. Suslov (4) was a student of Berg, the great Russian geographer, and his geography is clear, detailed, and extremely well illustrated. Parker (3) has an immense amount of useful information and many excellent sketch maps.

(1) Barthold, V. V. *La Découverte de L'Asie: Histoire de l'Orienta-lisme en Europe et en Russie.* Translated by B. Nikitine. Paris, 1947.

(2) Kerner, R. J. *The Urge to the Sea: The Course of Russian His-*

tory: *The Role of Rivers, Portages, Ostrogs, Monasteries, and Furs.* Berkeley, 1946.
(3) Parker, W. H. *An Historical Geography of Russia.* Chicago, 1969.
(4) Suslov, S. P. *Physical Geography of Asiatic Russia.* Edited by J. Williams. Translated by N. D. Gershensky. San Francisco, 1961.

GENERAL BIBLIOGRAPHY

Mezhov (6) published many volumes of bibliography on Russian and Siberian history that are still fundamental references for works published up to the end of the nineteenth century. Kerner (5) continued this work for the period of, roughly, 1900 to 1937 and included publications in Chinese and Japanese.

(5) Kerner, R. J. *Northeastern Asia: A Selected Bibliography. Contributions to the Bibliography of the Relations of China, Russia, and Japan, with special reference to Korea, Manchuria, Mongolia, and Eastern Siberia, in Oriental and European Languages, Publication of the Northeastern Asia Seminar of the University of California.* 2 vols. Berkeley, 1939.
(6) Mezhov, V. *Russkaia istoricheskaia bibliografiia: ukazatel' knig i statei po russkoi i vseobshchei istorii i vspomogatel'nym naukam za 1800–1854 vkl* [Russian historical bibliography: A guide to books and articles of Russian and general history and the auxiliary sciences for the period 1800–1854]. St. Petersburg, 1892–1893.
(7) Mezhov, V. *Russkaia istoricheskaia bibliografiia za 1865–1876 g.g.* [Russian historical bibliography for 1865–1876]. 8 vols. in 4. St. Petersburg, 1882–1890.
(8) Mezhov, V. *Sibirskaia bibliografiia. Ukazatel' knig i statei o Sibiri na russkom iazyke i odnekh tol'ko knig na inostrannykh iazykakh za ves' period knigopechataniia* [Siberian bibliography. Guide to the books and articles on Siberia in Russian and foreign languages for the whole period of book printing]. 3 vols. in 2. St. Petersburg, 1903.
(9) Mezhov, V. *Supplement: Bibliographie des livres et articles russes de'histoire et sciences auxiliaires de 1800–1854.* 3 vols. St. Petersburg, 1892–1893.

THE GATHERING OF RUSSIA

Jettmar (18) gives an excellent general survey of the material works and peoples of the steppe country from the time of the Scythians to the Hsiung-nu. The text and the magnificent illustrations are indispensible for those who wish not only information but some feeling for the ancient land and its inhabitants. Gryaznov's work (15) is a splendidly illustrated general treatment of the prehistory (ca. 2300 B.C.–100 A.D.) of the Altai and Sayan areas and the steppe belt running between them. These two books together render a fine and authoritative overview of the Eurasian past.

The leading general histories of old Russia in Russian are those by Soloviëv (21) and Kliuchevskii (20). Kliuchevskii's works have been translated into English (19). Both Kliuchevskii and Soloviëv, particularly the latter, treated the history of Russia, properly, as that of an expanding state reacting to external pressures. The best histories of Russia in English were done by Russian scholars residing abroad. The first volume of Florinsky (11), which carries the history to the time of Alexander I, is the best single volume survey history in English. The four published volumes of Vernadsky (26), which come to the time of Ivan IV, are fine scholarship based on an exceedingly wide variety of sources.

On the Mongols and their conquest of Russia, Grousset's works (13, 14) are the best for the life and times of Ghengis Khan; Haenish (16) and Waley (27) have each translated the only known Mongol language chronicle. Haenish did a full and annotated translation of the text. Waley has no annotations and omits some of the duller genealogical material but produces an excellent and more graceful translation. A good short history of the Mongol Empire after Ghengis is by Grousset (14), and the best study is still that by D'Ohsson (10), which is preferable to the later extended study by Howarth (17). On the Mongol occupation of Russia refer to Vernadsky (26).

(1) D'Ohsson, C. *Histoire des Mongols depuis Tchinguiz khan jusqua Timour bey ou Tamerlane.* 4 vols. La Haye, Amsterdam, 1834–1835. An important source.
(11) Florinsky, M. *Russia: A History and an Interpretation.* 2 vols. New York, 1947, 1953.
(12) Grekov, B., and Yakubovskii, A *Zolotaia Orda i ee Padenine* [The Golden Horde and its Collapse and Fall]. Moscow, Leningrad, 1950.
(13) Grousset, R. *The Conqueror of the World.* Translated by Marian McKellar and Denis Sinor. New York, 1966.
(14) Grousset, R. *L'Empire des Steppes Attila, Ghengis-khan, Tamerlan.* Paris, 1939.
(15) Gryaznov, M. *South Siberia.* Geneva, 1969.
(16) Haenisch, E. *Die Geheime Geschichte der Mongolen, aus einer mongolischen Niederschrift des Jahres 1240 von der Insel Kode'im Kerulen Fluss, erstmalig übersetzt und erläütert.* Second edition. Leipzig, 1948.

(17) Howarth, H. *History of the Mongols From the 9th to the 19th Centuries.* 5 vols. London, 1876–1888. A vast amount of information, much of it of value, but in general inferior to (10) for the same period.

(18) Jettmar, K. *Art of the Steppes.* New York, 1967.

(19) Kliuchevskii, V. O. *History of Russia.* Translated by C. J. Hogarth. 5 vols. London and New York, 1911–1931.

(20) Kliuchevskii, V. O. *Kurs russkoi istorii* [The Course of Russian History]. 5 vols. Moscow, 1908.

(21) Soloviëv, S. M. *Istoriia Rossii s drevneishikh vremen* [History of Russia from Earliest Times]. 29 vols. in 7. St. Petersburg, 1894–1895.

(22) Spuler, B. *Die Goldene Horde, Die Mongolen in Russiland 1223–1502.* Leipzig, 1943.

(23) Vernadsky, G. *Ancient Russia.* New Haven, 1943. See for the steppe invasions the Avars, Sycthians, Khazars, Sarmatians, Goths. Note the bibliography.

(24) Vernadsky, G. *Kievan Russia.* New Haven, 1948. This is the best extant history of Russia in English from the ninth to the thirteenth century, fully footnoted and with an ample bibliography.

(25) Vernadsky, G. *The Mongols and Russia.* New Haven 1953. The best English language history for the period of the conquest, domination, and decline of the Golden Horde. The book has a very useful bibliography of sources, including Mongol, Turkish, Syriac, Arabic, Persian, Armenian, Georgian, Greek, and Latin, that gives one an idea of the area affected by the Mongol-Turkic conquest empire.

(26) Vernadsky, G. *Russia at the Dawn of the Modern Age.* New Haven, 1959. Russia in the sixteenth century and the Eastern policies of Ivan III and Vasili III (Kazan, Kasimov, Crimea) and the Novgorod struggle.

(27) Waley, A. *The Secret History of the Mongols and Other Pieces.* London, 1963.

In 1834 the Russian Academy of Sciences established an Archeographic Commission that gathered and published an enormous number of documentary sources on Russian and Siberian history which, in their entirety, constitute basic and indispensible source materials.

(28) Akademii nauk. Arkheograficheskaia kommissiia. *Akty istoricheskie* [Historical acts]. 5 vols. St. Petersburg, 1841–1842; Index, 1843.

132   *Bibliography*

(29) Akademii nauk. Arkheograficheskaia kommissiia. *Akty iuridicheskie* [Legal acts]. St. Petersburg, 1838.

(30) Akademii nauk. Arkhoegraficheskaia kommissiia. *Akty moskovskago gosudarstva* [Acts of the Muscovite state].

(31) Akademii nauk. Arkheograficheskaia kommissiia. *Akty sobrannye v bibliotekakh i arkhivakh rossiiskoi imperii arkheograficheskoi ekspeditsiei imperatorskoi akademii nauk* [Acts collected in the libraries and archives of the Russian empire by the Archeographic Expedition of the Imperial Academy of Sciences]. 4 vols. St. Petersburg, 1836. Index, St. Petersburg, 1838.

(32) Akademii nauk. Arkheograficheskaia kommissiia. *Dopolneniia k aktam istoricheskim* [Supplements to the historical acts]. 12 vols. (1150–1700) St. Petersburg, 1846–1872. Index (1–10) 1875.

(33) Akademii nauk. Arkheograficheskaia kommissiia. *Polnoe sobranie russikikh letopisei* [Complete collection of Russian chronicles]. 24 vols. in 11. St. Petersburg, 1841–1914.

(34) Akademii nauk. Arkheograficheskaia kommissiia. *Russkaia istoricheskaia biblioteka* [Russian historical library]. 39 vols. St. Petersburg, 1872–1927.

(35) Akademii nauk. Solostyennaia ego imperatorskago velichestva kantselioriia. *Pamiatniki diplomticheskikh snoshenii drevenei Rossii s derzhavami inostrannymi* [Memorials of the diplomatic relations of Old Russia with foreign powers]. 10 vols. St. Petersburg, 1851–1871.

(36) Akademii nauk. Solostyennaia ego imperatorskago velichestva kantselioriia. *Polnoe sobranie zakonov rossiiskoi imperii s 1649 goda* [Complete collections of laws of the Russian empire from 1649]. Series 1. 46 vols. in 48. St. Petersburg, 1830. Continued to 1916 in a total of 240 volumes.

(37) Bantysh-Kamenskii, N. N., et al., eds. *Sobranie gosudarstvennykh gramot i dogovorov, khraniashchikhsia v gosudarstvennoi kollegii inostrannykh del* [Collections of state charters and treaties preserved in the state college of foreign affairs]. 5 vols. Moscow, 1813–1894.

(38) Chernevskii, P. O. *Ukazatel' materialov dlia istorii torgovli, promyshlennosti i finansov v predelakh rossiiskoi imperii. Ot drevneishikh vremen do kontsa XVIII stoletiia* [Guide to the material for the history of trade, industry, and finance, within the limits of the Russian Empire, from earliest times to the end of the eighteenth century]. St. Petersburg, 1883.

THE MOVING FRONTIER–SIBERIA AND CENTRAL ASIA FROM THE CONQUEST OF SIBIR TO THE DEATH OF ALEXANDER I

In 1733 the Academy of Sciences commissioned an expedition to Siberia that included the historian Gerhard F. Mueller. Mueller spent ten years visiting every part of Siberia except Kamchatka and transcribing archival documents. He wrote a history of Siberia which was published in 1750 (71), with a second edition, the most commonly used, published in 1787. These two editions contain many manuscripts. A Russian edition of 1774 (52) done by J. E. Fischer is an abridgment, as is Fischer's German edition of 1768 (51). Mueller is a fundamental source. Mezhov's is a fundamental bibliography (8) for Siberian history to the nineteenth century. Golder (58), despite the title, closes at 1750 but is an important history in English based on Russian sources. Fischer (53), Lantzeff (67), Gibson (56), and Foust (55) are basic monographic studies and each has an excellent bibliography that should be consulted.

(39) Adelung, F. Von. *Kritiko-literaturnoe obozrenie puteshestvennikov po Rossii do 1700 goda i ikh sochinenii* [Critical literary survey of travelers to Russia up to 1700 and their works]. Translated from the German by Aleksandr Klevanov. In *Chteniia*, 1848, no. 9, pp. 1–104; 1863, no. 1 (January–March), pp. 105–174; 1863, no. 2 (April–June), pp. 185–305; 1863, no. 3 (July–September), pp. 1–86; 1863, no. 4 (October–December), pp. 87–168; 1864, no. 1 (January–March), pp. 169–264, i–v.

(40) Akademiia Nauk. Arkheograficheskaia kommissiia. *Pamiatniki sibirskoi istorii XVIII* [Records of Siberian history of the eighteenth century]. 2 vols. Vol. 1, 1700–1713; vol. 2, 1713–1724. St. Petersburg, 1882–1885.

(41) Akademiia Nauk. Arkheograficheskaia kommissiia. *Sibirskiia letopisi.* [Siberian chronicles]. St. Petersburg, 1907.

(42) Andreievich, V. K. *Istoriia Sibiri* [History of Siberia]. 5 vols. in 2. St. Petersburg, 1887–1889.

(43) Baer, K. F. *Der Verdienste Peter der Grossen um die Erweiterung der geographischen Kenntnisse.* Vol. 16 of *Beiträge zur Kenntnnis des russischen Reiches.* St. Petersburg, 1872.

(44) Bakhrushin, S. V. *Ocherki po istorii kolonizatsii Sibirii v XVI i XVII* [Outline of the colonization of Siberia in the sixteenth century and seventeenth century]. Moscow, 1927–1928. A good general history.

(45) Bakhrushin, S., and Tokarev, S., eds. *Yakutiia v XVII veke* [Yakutia in the seventeenth century] Yakutsk, 1953.

(46) Butsinskii, P. N. *Istoriia Sibiri: Surgut, Narymi Ketsk do 1645* [The history of Siberia: Surgut, Narym and Ketsk to 1645]. Kharkov, 1893.

(47) Chappe D'Auteroche. *A Journey into Siberia, Made by the order of the king of France.* Translated by T. Jeffreys. Second edition. London, 1774.

(48) Donnelly, A. *The Russian Conquest of Bashkiria 1552–1740: A Case Study in Imperialism.* New Haven, 1968. Russian policies and politics in the Kama-Volga-Ural rivers area.

(49) Drew, R. F. The emergence of an agricultural policy for Siberia in the XVII and XVIII centuries." *Agricultural History* 33 (1959):29–39.

(50) Firsov, N. N. *Chteniia po istorii Sibiri* [Readings on the history of Siberia]. 2 vols. in 1. Moscow, 1920–1921.

(51) Fischer, J. E. *Siberische Geschichte von der Entdeckung Sibiriens bis auf die Eroberung dieses Landes durch die russischen Waffe.* 2 vols. St. Petersburg, 1768.

(52) Fischer, J. E. *Sibirskaia istoriia ot samago otkrytiia Sibiri do zavoevaniia sei zemli rossiiskim oruzhiem* [Siberian history from the first discovery of Siberia to the complete conquest of this land by Russian arms]. St. Petersburg, 1774.

(53) Fisher, Raymond. *The Russian Fur Trade 1550–1700.* Berkeley, 1943.

(54) Fletcher, G. and Horsey, Sir J. *Russia at the Close of the Sixteenth Century, Comprising the Treaties "Of the Russe Common Wealth" by Dr. Giles Fletcher; and the Travels of Sir Jerome Horsey, Knt.* Edited by Edward A. Bond. Hakluyt Society Works, vol. XX. London, 1856.

(55) Foust, C. *Muscovite and Mandarin: Russia's Trade with China and its Setting 1727–1805.* Chapel Hill, 1969. On the Kiakhta trade. A valuable and informative study.

(56) Gibson, J. *Feeding the Russian Fur Trade: Provisionment of the Okhotsk Seaboard and the Kamchatka Peninsula 1639–1856.* Madison, 1969. Exceptionally capable study in history and geography. Well illustrated.

(57) Gmelin, J. G. *Travels through Siberia, between the years 1733–1743.* 4 vols. Harlem, 1752–1757.

(58) Golder, F. *Russian Expansion in the Pacific 1641–1850.* Cleveland, 1914.

(59) Golovachev, P. M., ed. *Tomsk v XVII veke* [Tomsk in the seventeenth century]. St. Petersburg, 1907.

(60) Henning, G. "Die Reiseberichte über Sibirien von Herberstein bis Ides" in *Mitteilungen des Vereins für Erdkunde zu Leipzig, 1905.* Leipzig, 1906.

(61) Herberstein, S. von, et al. *Notes upon Russia: Being a Transla-tion of the Earliest Account of that Country, Entitled Rerum Moscovitarum Commentarii, by the Baron Sigismund von Herberstein.* Translated and edited by R. H. Major. 2 vols. Hakluyt Society Works, vols. X and XII, London, 1851–1852.

(62) Irkutsk. *Materialy dlia istorii goroda* [Materials for a history of the city of Irkutsk]. Moscow, 1883.

(63) Kaidanov, N. *Sistematicheskii katalog delam sibirskago prikaza* [Systematic catalogue of the transactions of the Siberian Prikaz]. St. Petersburg, 1888.

(64) Katanaev, G. *Kratkii istoricheskii obzor sluzhby sibirskago kazach'ego voiska s 1582 po 1908* [Brief historical survey of the service of the Siberian Cossack Army 1582–1908]. St. Petersburg, 1908.

(65) Kuznetsov, E. *Sibirskii letopisets, Letopis kontsa XVII i nachala XVIII stoletii, vedennaia v Tobolskye* [Annals of Siberia: Annals of the seventeenth and the beginning of the eighteenth century from the archives of Tobolsk]. Tobolsk, 1892.

(66) Kuznetsov-Krasnoiarskii, I., comp. *Istoricheskie akty XVII stoletiia (1633–1699). Materially dlia istorii Sibiri* [Historical acts of the seventeenth century (1633–1699). Material for the history of Siberia]. 2 vols., Tomsk, 1890–1897.

(67) Lantzeff, George. *Siberia in the Seventeenth Century: A Study of the Colonial Administration.* Berkeley, 1943.

(68) Levin, M., and Potapov, L., eds. *Istoriko-etnograficheski'atlas Sibiri* [An historical and ethnographic atlas of Siberia]. Moscow and Leningrad, 1961.

(69) Levin, M., and Potapov, L. *The Peoples of Siberia.* Chicago, 1964. Published in Moscow as *Narody Sibirii* in 1956.

(70) Messerschmidt, D. *Forschungsreise durch Sibirien 1720–1727. Teil 4, Tagebuch Aufzeichnung Februar 1725–November 1725.* Edited by Winter, Uschman, and Jarosch. Berlin, 1968. During the period covered by this portion of Messerschmidt's diary, he and his party traveled from Samarov on the Ob to Udinsk west of Lake Baikal along the Ob, Ket, Stoney Tunguska, and Angara rivers.

(71) Mueller, G. F. *Conquest of Siberia and the history of the trans-actions, wars, commerce, etc. carried on between Russia and China, from the earliest period.* Translated from the Russian of G. F. Mueller and of P. S. Pallas, London, 1842.

(72) Mueller, G. F. *Istoriia Sibiri* [History of Siberia]. A one-volume revision of the following (73). Moscow, Leningrad, 1937.

(73) Mueller, G. F. *Opisanie sibirskago tsarstva i vsekh proizshed-skikh v nem del ot nachala, a osoblivo ot pokoreniia ego rossiiskoi derzhave po sii vremena* [Description of the Siberian kingdom and all events occurring there from the beginning but especially from its subjugation to Russian power up to the present]. First edition, St. Petersburg, 1750.

(74) Mueller, G. F. *Sammlung Russischer Geschichte*. 9 vols. in 8. St. Petersburg, 1732–1764. Mueller was the great archivist of Siberian history. He arrived in Russia in 1725 and joined Bering's first expedition (although he did not go to sea). From 1733–1743 he collected and copied archival materials in Siberia. The materials he collected are in thirty-eight stout volumes known as "Mueller's Portfolios" and are preserved in Leningrad and Moscow. Many of these manuscripts are still unpublished. Mueller published a goodly number in the volumes of the *Sammlung Russischer Geschichte*. There is a spurious edition of this with the same title edited by J. H. Merk and published in Offenbach am Main (1777–1779). A great deal of the *Sammlung* was translated as the *Beiträge zur Kenntniss Russlands und seiner Geschichte* (edited by G. Evers and M. von Engelhardt) begun in Dorpat, 1818, as a periodical and in the *Beiträge zur Kenntniss des Russischen Reiches und der Angrezenden Länden Asiens*, started by K. von Baer (Bayer) as an occasional journal for the Academy of Sciences. Of particular interest in the *Sammlung* are: volume 3, parts 5 and 6, on the Siberian trade; volume 6, parts 2–6, on the history of Siberia; volume 8, parts 1–5, on the history of Siberia, and volume 8, part 6, on the Russo-Chinese trade.

(75) Ogloblin, N. *Obozrenie stolbtsov i knig sibirskago prikaza, 1592–1768.* g.g. [Survey of the rolls and books of the Siberian Prikaz, 1592–1768]. 4 vols. Moscow, 1896–1900.

(76) Ogorodnikov, V. I. *Iz istorii pokoreniia Sibiri. Pokorenie iuka-girskoi zemli* [From the history of the Siberian conquest. The conquest of the land of the Iukagirs]. Chita, 1922.

(77) Pallas, P. S. *Neue Nordische Beyträge zur physikalischen und geographischen Erd-und Völkerbeschreibung Naturges-chichte und Oekonomie*. 7 vols. St. Petersburg and Leipzig, 1781–1796.

(78) Raeff, M. *Siberia and the Reform of 1822*. Seattle, 1956.

(79) Remezov, S. *Chertezhnaia kniga Sibiri* [Atlas of Siberia]. St. Petersburg, 1882. A reprint of an atlas compiled by Remezov at the order of Moscow in 1690.

(80) Serebrennikov, I. N. *Pokorenie i pervonachal'noe zaselenie Irkutskoi gubernii* [Conquest and first settlement of the Irkutsk gubernia]. Irkutsk, 1883.

(81) *Siberskie goroda. Materialy dlia ikh istorii xvii stoletii. Nerchinsk, Seleniginsk, Yakutsk* [Siberian towns. Materials for the history of the seventeenth and eighteenth centuries: Nerchinsk, 'Selenginsk, Yakutsk]. Moscow, 1886.

(82) Slovtsov, P. *Istoricheskoye obozrenie Sibiri* [Survey of Siberian History]. 2 vols. in 1. St. Petersburg, 1886.

(83) Titov, A., ed. *Sibir' v XVII veke, Sbornik starinnykh russkikh statei o Sibiri i prilezhashchikh k ne i zemliakh* [Siberia in the seventeenth century. A collection of old Russian accounts of Siberia and the lands bordering it]. Moscow, 1890.

CENTRAL ASIA

Because of its complex of peoples, many of whom were without writing, and because of its amorphous boundaries, there has been no general history of the area from the Caspian Sea to the Altai Mountains, but there are several good guides and bibliographies. Sinor (92) calls his work "a guide to the immense literature of the languages, history, and ethnography of Central Eurasia." It is, in addition, a most comprehensive, well-organized, and intelligently annotated bibliography. Very little of it, except parts of the third section, bears directly on the matter of Siberian history, but it is, in general, of great value for the history of the peoples of Central Eurasia. Courant's (87) bibliography is useful for the internal struggles and divisions of the tribes and khanates. All of V. V. Barthold's fundamental works on Turkestan have been translated and should be read by anyone with a serious interest in Turkish Central Asia (84, 85, and 86). For the ethnology of the region, Czaplica (88) is a standard study. The Skrine and Ross book (94) is important because of its scope—from the earliest times to the nineteenth century—and partly for its use of Arabic and Persian sources. Veselovski (95) compiled the basic documents on Russo-Persian relations. Of all of the contemporary accounts, two stand out: Jenkinson's, for his description of Astrakhan and the Caspian trade and Bokhara in the sixteenth century (89), and Schuyler's (91), for his firsthand look at Turkestan in the nineteenth century.

(84) Barthold, V. V. *Four Studies on the History of Central Asia.* Translated by V. and T. Minorsky. Vol. 1, Leiden, 1956.

(85) Barthold, V. V. *Histoire des Turks d'Asie Centrale.* Translated by M. Donskis. Paris, 1945.

(86) Barthold, V. V. *Turkestan at the Time of the Mongol Invasion.* Translated by D. Ross. Oxford, 1918.

(87) Courant, M. *L'Asie Centrale aux XVIIe et XVIIIe siecles: Empire kalmouk ou Empire Mantchow.* Lyon-Paris, 1912.

(88) Czaplica, M. *The Turks of Central Asia in History and at the Present Day.* Oxford, 1918.

(89) Jenkinson, Anthony, et al. *Early Voyages and Travels to Russia and Persia. With Account of the First Intercourse of the English with Russia and Central Asia, by way of the Caspian Sea.* Edited by E. Delmar Morgan and C. H. Coote. 2 vols. Hakluyt Society Works, vols. 72–73. London, 1886.

(90) Lattimore, O. *Inner Asian Frontiers of China.* American Geographical Society: Research Series no. 21, 1939. The first 251 pages are of particular interest for a grasp of the overall problems of the land frontiers of China.

(91) Schuyler, E. Turkistan: *Note of a Journey in Russian Turkistan, Kokand, Bukhara and Koldja.* Abridged edition. Edited by K. West, with an introduction by Geoffrey Wheeler. New York, 1966.

(92) Sinor, D. *Inner Asia: History, Civilization, Languages: A syllabus.* Bloomington, Indiana, 1969. Designed as a compact guide for teachers. There is one chapter on Russia in Asia.

(93) Sinor, D. *Introduction a l'Étude de l'Eurasia Centrale.* Wiesbaden, 1963.

(94) Skrine, F. H., and Ross, E. D. *The Heart of Asia: A History of Russian Turkestan and the Central Asian Khanates from the Earliest Times.* London, 1899.

(95) Veselovskii, N., comp. *Pamiatniki diplomaticheskikh i torgovykh snoshenii moskovskoi Rusi s Persiei* [memorials of diplomatic and commercial relations of Muscovite Russia with Persia]. 3 vols. In *Trudy vostochnago otdelniia imperatorskago russkago arkheologischeskago obshchestva.* Vols. 20–22. St. Petersburg, 1890–1898.

RUSSIA AND CHINA

One who is capable of using the Chinese language sources noted below needs no instruction on the nature and use of Chinese written history. For those unfamiliar with Chinese historiography and Chinese sources, however, official and unofficial, items (96, 97, and 98) will be of interest and use.

(96) Gardner, C. S. *Chinese Traditional Historiography.* Cambridge, 1938. Less of a guide and more of an insight into the mind and motives of traditional historians.

(97) Han, Y. *Elements of Chinese Historiography.* Hollywood, 1955. Clear and well-organized guide to the types, categories, and nomenclature of Chinese history.

(98) Knoblock, J. "Chinese Historiography" in *The Carrell* (journal of the Friends of the University of Miami Library). Vol. 10, June, 1969.

(99) Baddeley, J. F. *Russia, Mongolia, China: Being Some Record of the Relations between them from the beginning of the XVI Century to the Death of the Tsar Alexei Mikhailovitch A.D. 1602–1676; Rendered mainly in the form of Narratives dictated or written by the Envoys sent by the Russian Tsars, or their Voevodas in Siberia to the Kalmuck and Mongol Khans and Princes and to the Emperors of China, with Introductions, historical and geographical also A Series of Maps showing the Progress of Geographical knowledge in regard to Northern Asia during the XVI, XVII and early XVIII centuries: The Text taken more especially from the MSS in the Moscow Foreign Office Archives with Extensive Indexes.* Twenty-seven maps, numerous illustrations in the text, facsimiles, and tables of pedigrees. 2 vols. London, 1919. A source of immense value.

(100) Bakhrushin, S. *Kazaki na Amure* [Cossacks on the Amur]. Leningrad, 1925.

(101) Bannikov, A. *Pervye russkie puteshestviia v Mongoliiu i Severnyi Kitai* [The first Russian travelers into Mongolia and North China]. Moscow, 1954. Accounts of the trips of Baikov, Petlin, and Tiumenets.

(102) Bantysh-Kamenski, N. *Diplomaticheskoe sobranie del mezhdu Rossiskim i kitaiskim gosudarstvami s 1619 po 1792 god* [Collection of diplomatic matters between the Russian and Chinese governments, 1619–1792]. Kazan, 1882. Excellent sources prepared by the Chief of the Archives who succeeded Mueller.

(103) Bell, J. *Travels from St. Petersburg in Russia to Divers Parts of Asia.* 2 vols. London, 1764. Bell was a Scotch physician in Russian service who, between 1715 and 1722, accompanied Russian missions to Persia, China, and Central Asia.

(104) Berton, P., comp. *Soviet Works on China: A Bibliography of Nonperiodical Literature 1946–1955.* Los Angeles, 1959. Valuable for its listing of Soviet doctoral dissertation ab-

stracts and for the listing of a small number of important Soviet works on Siberia that were issued in very limited quantities.

(105) Brand, A. *A Journal of the Embassy from their Majesties John and Peter Alexievitz, Emperors of Muscovy. Overland into China, through the Provinces of Ustugha, Siberia, Dauri, and the Great Tartary to Peking, the Capital City of the Chinese Empire. By Everard Isbrand, their Ambassador in the Years 1693, 1694, and 1695.* London, 1698.

(106) Bretschneider, E. *Medieval Researches from East Asiatic Sources towards the Knowledge of the Geography and History of Central and Western Asia from the 13th to the 17th centuries.* 2 vols. London, 1910. Useful source for Chinese relations with Central Asia and with the Mongols.

(107) Cahen, G. *Histoire des relations de la Russie avec la Chine sous Pierre Le Grand 1689–1730.* Paris, 1912. The text is translated in full with additional materials by W. Shelden Ridge as *Some Early Russo-Chinese Relations.* Shanghai, 1914. Somewhat of a digest but interesting and useful.

(108) Cha Chi-tso. *Tsui-wei lu* [A complete history of the Ming dynasty]. Shanghai, 1928. A history critical of the Manchus and therefore not published until long after the author's death.

(109) Chang Hsing-lang. *Chung hsi chiao-tung shih-liao hu-pen* [Materials for a study of the relations of China with other countries]. 6 vols. Peiping, 1930. Volume 5 covers Central Asia.

(110) *Ch'ing tai wai chiao shih liao.* Diplomatic documents of the Ching dynasty. Peiping, 1932.

(111) Ch'u Yun-shih. *Fan-pu yao-lüeh* [History of the Mongol Frontier]. An eighteenth-century compilation of much interest.

(112) Chuldov, N. P. "Erofei Pavlov Khabarov: dobytchik i pribyl'nik XVII veka" [Erofei Pavlov Khabarov: freebooter and profiteer of the seventeenth century] in *Russkii arkhiv.* 1898, no. 2, pp. 177–190.

(113) Cordier, H. *Bibliotheca Sinica.* Second edition, revised. 4 vols. Paris, 1904–1908. Suppl. vol. 5, Paris, 1921. Quite comprehensive on Western (including Russian) language books to 1921. Topical arrangement.

(114) Franke, W. "Yunglos Mongolei-Feldzüge" in *Sinologische Arbeiten.* Vol. 3 (1945), pp. 1–45.

(115) Fu Lo-shu, comp., ed., and trans. *A Documentary Chronicle of Sino-Western Relations (1644–1820).* 2 vols. Tucson, 1966. The first volume is a series of translations of valu-

able materials from Chinese archives and histories. The second volume of notes and annotations is poorly organized but a rich mine of information.

(116) Ho Ch'iu-t'ao. *Shuo-fang pei-sh'eng* [Historical source book of the northern regions]. This is the first official account of the campaigns against the Russians between 1682–1689. It was presented to the throne in 1860 and was published in 1881.

(117) Hsiao I-shan. *Ch'ing-tai t'ung shih* [Comprehensive history of the Ch'ing dynasty]. 2 vols. Shanghai, 1927–1928. Revised edition, 5 vols. Taipei, 1963. See volume 1, sections 5 and 6, chapters 22–25 for Russian relations. In many respects this is the best history of the era.

(118) *Huang ch'ao Fan-shu yü-ti Ts'ung shu* [Collection of geographical studies on the Imperial Dependencies and Divisions]. Shanghai, 1903.

(119) Hudson, G. *Europe and China: A Survey of Their Relations from the Earliest Times to 1800.* London, 1931. This good survey is most useful in understanding the Russian relationships as part of a larger relation with Europe.

(120) Hummel, A., ed. *Eminent Chinese of the Ch'ing Period.* 2 vols. Washington, 1943–1944. Cross reading of the appropriate biographies in this superb work will illuminate the entire course of Ch'ing history (1644–1912).

(121) Ides, E. Y. *Three Years Travel from Moscow Overland to China; through Great Ustigia, Siriana, Permia, Daour, Great Tartary, . . . to Peking . . . London, 1706.* This account of Ides was anticipated by A. Brand, who published an inconsistent account of Ides' journey in 1697. The Ides account is more easily found in abriged form in J. Harris, *A Complete Collection of Voyages and Travels.* 2 vols. London, 1764. Vol. 2, pp. 918–961.

(122) Klaproth, M. J., ed. *Voyage in Peking, a travers la mongolie en 1820 et 1821 par M. C. Timkovski.* Paris, 1827.

(123) Korsak, A. *Istoriko-statisticheskoe obozrenie torgovykh snoshenii Rossii s Kitaem* [Historical-statistical survey of the trade relations of Russia with China]. Kazan, 1857.

(124) Lange, L. "Journal of the Residence of Mr. DeLange, Agent of His Imperial Majesty of all the Russias, Peter the First, at the Court of Peking, during the years 1721 and 1722" in John Bell, *Travels from St. Petersburg in Russia to Divers Parts of Asia. . . .* Glasgow, 1763. More easily found in volume 7 of John Pinkerton's *A General Collection of the Best and Most Interesting Travels.* London, 1811.

(125) Lattimore, O. *Studies in Frontier History: Collected Papers 1928–1958.* New York, 1962. Note especially pages 134–149, "Chinese and Russian Margins of Expansion."

(126) *Li-fan-yuan tse-li* [Collected Institutes of the Li-fan-yuan]. New and revised edition, 1843.

(127) Lust, J., and Eichorn, W. *Index Sinicus, A Catalogue of articles relating to China in periodicals and other collective publications 1920–1955.* Cambridge, 1964. Has author and subject index.

(128) Mancall, M. "China's First Missions to Russia, 1729–1731" in *Papers on China.* Harvard University Committee on Regional Studies. Vol. 9 (1955), pp. 75–110. Short interesting account of China's diplomatic effort to block the Kalmucks.

(129) Naitō Torajiro, ed. *Man-Mō sōsho* [Collectanea on Manchuria and Mongolia]. 7 vols. Tokyo, 1919–1922. *Inter alia* there is much information on Manchu-Mongol and Chinese-Mongol relations.

(130) Pallas, S. P. *Sammlungen historischer Nachrichten über die mongolischen Völkerschaften.* 2 vols. St. Petersburg, 1776–1801.

(131) Pavlovsky, M. "La Chine et la Russie en Asie Centrale" in *Bulletin de l'Universite l'Aurore.* Vol. 6 (1948), pp. 312–325.

(132) Pavlovsky, M. "La Mongolie dans les relations sino-russe" in *Bulletin de l'Universite l'Aurore.* No. 3 (1944).

(133) Potapov, L. P. *Ocherk istorii Oirotii. Altaitsy v period russkoi kolonizatsii* [Essay on the history of Oirotia. The Altai natives during the period of Russian colonization]. Novosibirsk, 1933.

(134) "Puteshestvie chrez Sibir'ot Tobol'ska do Nerchinska i granits Kitaia russkago poslannika Nikolaia Spafariia v 1675 godu" [Journey across Siberia from Tobolsk to Nerchinsk and the borders of China of the Russian ambassador Nikolai Spafarii in 1675], in *Zapiski imperatorskago russkago geograficheskago obshchestva po otdeleniiu etnografii.* Vol. 10 (1882), pp. 1–214. St. Petersburg.

(135) Ravenstein, E. G. *The Russians on the Amur.* London, 1861.

(136) Rockhill, W. "The Dalai Lamas of Lhasa and Their Relations with the Manchu Emperors of China, 1644–1908." *T'oung Pao.* Vol. 2 (1910), pp. 41–104.

(137) Sebes, J. *The Jesuits and The Sino-Russian Treaty of Nerchensk (1689). The Diary of Thomas Pereira S. J. Rome.* 1961. Pages 1–75 contain a well-written summary of Russo-Chinese relations to 1689.

(138) Serruys, H. *Sino-Mongol Relations during the Ming: II. The Tribal System and Diplomatic Missions (1400–1600).* Melanges Chinois et Bouddhiques. Vol. 14. Bruxelles, 1967. An interesting and carefully researched study of Chinese-Mongol relations that had influence on later Chinese-Mongol-Russian relations.

(139) Shastino, N. *Russko-Mongol'skie posol'skie otnosheniz XVII veka* [Russian-Mongol Diplomatic Relations during the seventeenth century]. Moscow, 1958.

(140) Skachkov, P. *Bibliografiia Kitaia* [Bibliography of China]. Lists books and periodical articles in Russian for the period 1730–1930. Moscow, 1932. Ann Arbor, 1948.

(141) "Stateinyi spisok posol'stva N. Spafariia v Kitai" [Detailed account of the embassy of N. Spafarii to China] in *Vestnik arkheologii i istorii.* Vol. 17 (1906), pp. 162–339. St. Petersburg.

(142) *Ta-Ch'ing i-t'ung shih* [Comprehensive Geography of the Ch'ing Empire]. 1843.

(143) "The Travels of Feodore Iskowitz Baikhof from Moscow into China (1654–1656)" in Awnshem and John Churchill's *A Collection of Voyages and Travels.* London, 1704. Vol. 2, pp. 469–473.

(144) Tseng Wen-wu. *Chung-kuo ching-ying hsi-yü shih* [History of the Chinese expansion into and colonization of the Sinkiang area]. Shanghai, 1936. Although Chinese Turkestan did not become the province of Sinkiang until 1882, this history treats in detail the earlier period.

(145) Tsou Tai-chun. *Chung-O chieh chi* [On the boundaries between Russia and China]. 2 vols. Wuchang, 1911.

(146) Wei Yuan. *Shih-i-ch'ao sheng-wu chi* [The military operations of the Ch'ing dynasty to the Tao-kuang era]. Reprint, 1875.

(147) Yuan, T. L. *China in Western Literature. A Continuation of Cordier's Bibliotheca Sinica.* New Haven, 1958. Covers books and monographs in English, French, German, and Portuguese for the period 1921–1957. For the period since 1957 the annual bibliographical supplements of the *Journal of Asian Studies* should be used.

(148) Yuan, T. L. *Russian Works on China 1918–1960 in American Libraries.* New Haven, 1961.

THE NORTH PACIFIC AND NORTH AMERICA

(149) U.S. Coast and Geodetic Survey, *Pacific Coast Pilot: Coast and Islands of Alaska: Second Series.* Washington, 1879.

144   *Bibliography*

Pages 225 to 375 are entitled "A partial list of Books, Pamphlets and other publications on Alaska and adjacent regions compiled by W. H. Dall and Marcus Baker." Dall, the senior compiler, spent years in archival research including the archives in Saint Petersburg. The result is a little known but amazingly complete listing of publications on the history and exploration of Siberia, the North Pacific, and the Northwest Coast. Especially valuable are the listings of the papers and publications of the Russian Imperial Geographic Society, The Russian Hydrographic Office, The Russian Ministry of Foreign Affairs, and the Committee on the Organization of the Russian-American Company.

(150) Andreiev, A., ed. *Russkie otkyiia v Tikhom okeane i Severnoi Amerike v XVIII veke.* Moscow, 1948. Translated by C. Ginsburg as *Russian Discoveries in the Pacific and in North America in the Eighteenth and Nineteenth Centuries.* Ann Arbor, 1952.
(151) Berg, L. *Ocherki po istorii Russkikh geograficheskikh otkrytii* [Essays on the history of Russian geographical discoveries]. Moscow and Leningrad, 1946. A compact survey by a great geographer.
(152) Berg, L. *Otkrytie Kamchatki i ekspeditsii Beringa* [The Discovery of Kamchatka and the expeditions of Bering]. Third edition. Moscow and Leningrad, 1946.
(153) Coxe, W. *Account of the Russian Discoveries between Asia and America to which are added the Conquest of Siberia and the History of Transactions and Commerce between Russia and China.* Fourth edition. London, 1803. Coxe collected the journals of all the voyages between 1711 and 1792, translated them into English, and arranged them as a narrative sequence. He worked in St. Petersburg and consulted with Mueller. His account is the best English source.
(154) Golder, F. A. *Berings Voyages: An Account of the Effort of the Russians to determine the Relation of America and Asia.* 2 vols. New York, 1922. Volume 1 contains the log books and official reports of the expeditions of 1725–1730 and 1733–1742. Volume 2 contains Steller's journals of the voyage from Kamchatka to America and return in 1741–1742, as well as a bibliography of the accounts of participants in Bering's voyages.
(155) Golder, F. A. *Guide to Materials for American History in Russian Archives.* Carnegie Institution Publication no. 239. Washington, 1917. A list of all the—to that time—

unpublished materials in the archives of St. Petersburg and Moscow.

(156) Greenhow, R. *Memoir, Historical and Political of the North-west Coast of North America and Adjacent Territories.* Washington, 1840. An important review of the dis-coveries in Alaska based on documents.

(157) Krasnennikov, *Opisanie Zemli Kamchatki.* St. Petersburg, 1754. Translated in English by J. Grieve as *The History of Kamtschatka and the Kuriliski Islands with The Coun-tries Adjacent: Illustrated with Maps and Cuts.* Glocester, 1764. The original is a good firsthand account. The English translation omits about one-fourth of the original and the remainder is of poor quality. A good but in-complete French translation is found in volume 2 of C. d'Auteroche's *Voyage en Siberie.* Paris. 1768.

(158) Sauer, M. *An Account of a Geographical and Astronomical Expedition to the Northern Parts of Russia at the Com-mand of Catherine II, Performed by Captain Joseph Bill-ings, 1785-1794.* London, 1802. Extracted from the log of Billings' sailing master, Lachov.

(159) Sokolov, A. *Russkaia Morskaia Biblioteka 1701-1851* [Russian Marine Library 1701-1851]. Second edition. St. Peters-burg, 1882. A very good listing of the Russian literature of discovery by sea.

(160) Wickersham, J. *A Bibliography of Alaskan Literature 1724-1924.* Cordova, Alaska, 1927. Wickersham was a pioneer of Alaska and an amateur of its history who devoted much of his life to acquiring a library and compiling a catalog of Alaskan literature. W. H. Dall, who saw the card catalog years before its completion, called it "aston-ishingly thorough" for its coverage. Entries are in En-glish, Russian, German, French, and Spanish.

THE RUSSIAN-AMERICAN COMPANY

Part of the agreement of the sale of Alaska was that the correspon-dence, accounts, and archives of the Russian-American Company in Alaska become the property of the U.S. government. As a result, the Library of Congress has 182 volumes of materials of the company. These have not been exploited, partly due to lack of interest and partly due to the enormous difficulty of reading scrawled, hand-written Russian of the late eighteenth and early nineteenth centuries.

(161) Chevigny, H *Lord of Alaska: Baronov and the Russian Ad-venture.* London, 1946.

(162) Chevigny, H. *Lost Empire, The Life and adventures of Nikolai Petrovich Rezanov.* New York, 1937.

(163) Chevigny, H. *Russian America, The Great Alaskan Adventure, 1741–1867.* New York, 1965.

(164) Okun', S. *Rossiiskoe-amerikanskaia kompaniia* [The Russian-American Company]. Moscow and Leningrad, 1939. An excellent history with a Soviet point of view on the "imperialistic" and "capitalistic" nature of the company. Ably translated by C. Ginsberg as *The Russian-American Company.* Cambridge, 1951.

(165) Russel, T., ed. *The Rezanov Voyage to Nueva California in 1806.* San Francisco, 1926. Based on Rezanov's reports to the Minister of Commerce in St. Petersburg.

(166) Sheffer, I. "Les Russes aux Isles Hawaii 1816–1818." MS no. 59181 in Pinart's Collection at the Bancroft Library of the University of California in Berkeley. The complete story of the Russian attempt to establish a naval station in Hawaii.

(167) Tikhmenev, P. *Istoricheskoe obozenie Obrazovania rossiisko-amerikanskoi Kompani i diestvii eia do nastoishchago vremeni* [Historical Survey of the founding of the Russian-American Company and its history to the present time]. 2 vols. St. Petersburg, 1861–1863. A most valuable text and documentation. Volume 2 contains the correspondence of Rezanov.

RUSSIA AND JAPAN

(168) Harrison, J. *Japan's Northern Frontier.* Gainesville, 1953. Appendix one, "The Discovery of Yezo," describes all western voyages in Northern Japanese waters during the seventeenth and eighteenth centuries and contains an annotated bibliography of the literature of voyages in the North Pacific from 1596 to 1811.

(169) Kerner, R. J. "Russian Expansion to America: its Bibliographical Foundations" in *The Papers of the Bibliographical Society of America.* Vol. 25 (1931), pp. 111–129.

(170) Lensen, G. *The Russian Push Toward Japan: Russo-Japanese Relations 1697–1895.* Princeton, 1959. This work covers the subject of Russo-Japanese relations in the Kuriles and Hokkaido so well and uses both Japanese and Russian secondary sources so extensively that it has no peer for the subject. It has a bibliography that is particularly useful for its citation of numerous articles from Russian and Japanese learned journals.

(171) Okamoto, Ryonosuke. *Nichi-Ro kosho Hokkaido shiko* [Hokkaido historical documents concerning Russo-Japanese Relations]. 2 vols. Tokyo, 1898.

(172) Pozdneev, D. *Materialy po istorii severnoi Iaponii i eia otnoshenii k materiku Azii i Rossii* [Materials concerning the history of Northern Japan and her relations to the mainland of Asia and Russia]. 2 vols. Tokyo, 1909.

(173) Skalkovsie, K. *Russkaia torgovlia v tikhom okeane* [Russian trade in the Pacific Ocean]. St. Petersburg, 1883.

(174) Tabohashi Kiyoshi. *Kindai Nihon gaikoku kankei-shi* [History of Japan's foreign relations in modern times]. Tokyo, 1930. A very well-written general history of Japan's modern foreign relations.

Index